HOW TO MAKE
POP-UP CARDS

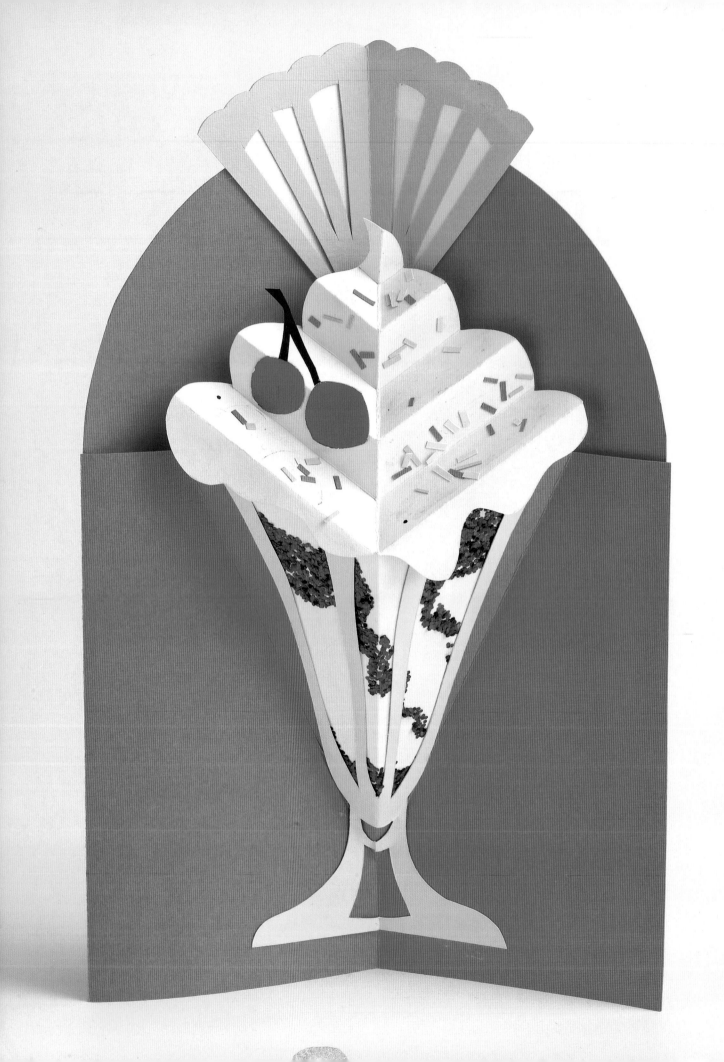

HOW TO MAKE POP-UP CARDS

55 PRACTICAL PROJECTS INCLUDING STEP-BY-STEP FOLDS

Suitable for beginners and experienced paper engineers, with
500 photographs showing every stage to ensure success

TRISH PHILLIPS & ANN MONTANARO

southwater

This edition is published by Southwater,
an imprint of Anness Publishing Ltd,
Blaby Road, Wigston, Leicestershire, LE18 4SE;

info@anness.com

www.southwaterbooks.com; www.annesspublishing.com

If you like the images in this book and would like to
investigate using them for publishing, promotions
or advertising, please visit our website
www.practicalpictures.com for more information.

Publisher: Joanna Lorenz
Project Editors: Daniel Hurst, Amy Christian
    and Kate Eddison
Photography: Paul Bricknell
Copy Editor: Beverley Jollands
Designer: Nigel Partridge
Production Controller: Wendy Lawson

© Anness Publishing Ltd 2013

Previously published as part of a larger volume,
*The Practical Step-by-Step Guide to Making Pop-ups
& Novelty Cards*

Contents

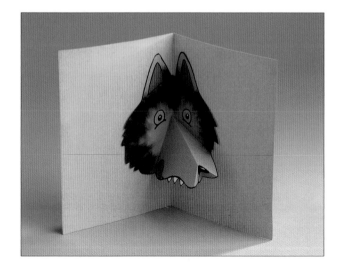

Introduction

Pop-up and movable cards and books have been used to delight, educate and celebrate for centuries, and their capacity to excite and amaze young and old alike has not diminished over time. Pop-ups are still as surprising and charming as ever, and the giddy thrill of turning the page of a story book and having a fairytale castle or a ferocious lion spring up is truly something to cherish.

This book offers the chance to master the secrets of the pop-up engineer and create your own magical pop-ups from scratch. Featuring a host of exciting techniques and projects this book is a wonderful introduction to making pop-up cards.

MATERIALS, TOOLS AND TECHNIQUES

The book begins with an introduction to the materials and tools that are available to the pop-up creator, such as scalpels and craft knives, glue and rulers. Paper and card are available in a confusing array of sizes and weights, and each is explained in turn along with a description of its suitability of use for your pop-ups.

▶ *A hand-made pop-up card will charm and delight the recipient.*

This section also examines basic techniques for cutting and folding, and looks at some of the potential problems that you may encounter when making your pop-ups. These techniques will form the basis of many of the projects in the book.

POP-UP PROJECTS

The main section of this book is dedicated to teaching practical techniques and projects that will help you create your own beautiful pop-ups at home. The projects are split into three chapters of varying difficulty, and each one is shown with clear instructions.

These techniques and projects are designed with a steady learning curve in mind, and each technique is explained in full before you are asked to implement it into an actual design. Learning the structure of each mechanism and the result it can achieve will help you to better understand what you are aiming for in the final design. It will also help you create your own unique designs from scratch at home.

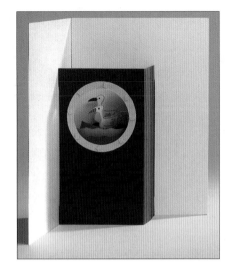

It is advisable to work your way through these chapters from the beginning, so that you have mastered all of the techniques required before you reach the advanced projects. If you follow the projects through from start to finish, you will have a myriad of seemingly intricate folds at your disposal that will allow you to plan your own designs that will surprise and delight your family and friends.

Don't be overwhelmed by the scale of any of the projects in this book, they are all achieved using simple techniques and can be easily mastered with patience and care. The most impressive looking projects require little more than accurate measuring and folding, plus a little creative flair from you. Above all, these projects are designed to be fun, both for the person who makes them and for anyone who is lucky enough to receive a beautifully crafted card.

◀ *Pop-ups bring stories to life, allowing characters to spring from the pages.*

▶ *Even the most complicated pop-up cards can be easily achieved with careful cutting and measuring.*

Paper and card

There is a seemingly infinite variety of options when it comes to choosing the materials for constructing your pop-up. The final choice will depend on whether you are making rough drafts or a finished piece, the size, and the intended durability of the piece.

PHOTOCOPY PAPER

Thin paper has the advantage of being cheap; a ream of 80–100gsm (grams per square metre) photocopy paper is very economical and is ideal for creating your first test pieces and experimenting on a small scale. An A5- or A6-sized sheet folded in half is perfect for practice runs, as it is smooth on both sides without any visible grain and creases easily. It is not a good choice for finished projects, however, as over time it can deteriorate, discolour and droop.

▼ *Paper and card (stock) comes in many sizes and thicknesses – the design you are making will dictate you choice.*

CARTRIDGE PAPER

This is suitable for final projects as it lasts longer than photocopy paper. It is worth buying acid-free, pH neutral paper as this prevents any yellowing and deterioration with age. The weight of cartridge paper varies from 96gsm to 220gsm. An ideal weight for small test pieces is 130gsm.

One downside to cartridge paper is that there is a noticeable grain on one side, so it is important to make

sure you fold your projects so that the smooth side is on the front of the design. Cartridge paper is available in a wide range of colours and comes in A1, A3 and A4 sizes.

CARD

Card (stock) sold in stationers is generally classified in three weights – thin, medium and thick. 300gsm is a good weight for large pop-ups. The pieces will be sturdy and long lasting, but the heavier the weight of card or paper, the more care is needed with creasing. Card is available in many exciting colours, but is generally only sold in A1, A3 or A4 sizes.

DECORATIVE PAPERS

When working on projects that would benefit from added colour or decoration there are many options available, but do bear in mind that complicated decorations can lessen the impact of the pop-up, and fussy patterns can flatten the image.

Simple white card used on its own is always very effective, and bright, uncomplicated colours work well, but pastels and intricate patterns will blend into the layers.

Card is rarely available in anything other than plain white, pastels and bright colours, although there are many types of decorative paper available. Good types to try are calligraphy paper, paper used for pastel drawing, slightly embossed papers, marbled papers and handmade papers. There are many beautiful handmade and decorated papers but it is always important to consider their suitability for cutting and folding.

PAPER AND CARD SIZE

The best size of paper and card to buy for general use is A3; this is easy to store, easy to cut down in size and very practical. Card is available in packs of A4 or single sheets of A1

and A3, and paper is available in all weights and sizes.

PAPER AND CARD STORAGE

Paper and card should be stored flat and never left rolled up for any length of time, as it is very difficult to get them perfectly flat again.

If you are using large sheets of paper regularly then you may want to invest in a plan chest, but this requires a large area. The easiest storage option is a large portfolio, which can be kept under the bed and out of the way. Although it is not ideal, it is possible to store pads upright (as they are bound on one edge and have a protective hard-backed cover), but always remember to store them with the spine uppermost, otherwise you will end up with a

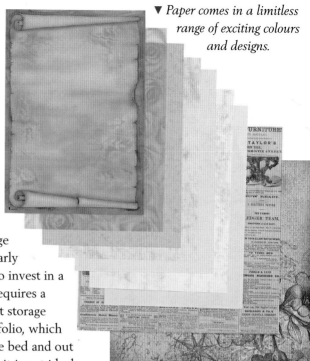

▼ *Paper comes in a limitless range of exciting colours and designs.*

ripple effect throughout the whole pad, rendering the card or paper unusable. It is important not to store card and paper in direct sunlight as this will fade it, especially those that are brightly coloured. It is also crucial that you do not store your card and paper in a damp environment, such as a garage, as this will cause warping and can lead to the formation of mildew.

WHERE TO BUY

Basic card and paper is available in many places; stationers, art shops and even supermarkets often have a stationery department. There are now many craft and hobby superstores which offer a huge choice of more specialist decorated and handmade papers, with the added bonus of many other essential tools as well.

◄ *Decorative papers can add interest to a design, but can also serve to flatten and detract from the overall impact of a pop-up.*

Tools and equipment

Before you embark on the projects in this book it is important to ensure that you have access to the right tools for the job. These are relatively inexpensive, but will prove invaluable for pop-up projects and for other crafts.

CUTTING MAT

The surface of a cutting mat is self-healing and smooth, so a good mat should last you a long time. Economizing by using cardboard or wood is an option, but the surface quickly gets ruined which can result in uneven and crooked cuts. A2- or A3-sized mats are ideal, and should be large enough for all of your projects. Cutting mats are not just for cutting but also for measuring – they are usually marked in a grid of 1cm squares, which allows for some easy measuring shortcuts. Simply align two edges of the page to the grid and you can draw perfectly straight and parallel lines using the squares on the mat as a guide, or cut 90° angles quickly without using a protractor or set square.

SCALPELS & CRAFT KNIVES

A scalpel gives the greatest control and precision, but craft knives and disposable scalpels make good alternatives. It is important to make sure that you have a ready supply of new blades, as a blunt blade is ineffectual and can tear your paper.

▼ *The essential tools for making pop-ups are a cutting mat, metal ruler, scalpel, embossing tool, bone folder, pencil, compass, eraser, pencil sharpener, set square, protractor, glue and low-tack masking tape.*

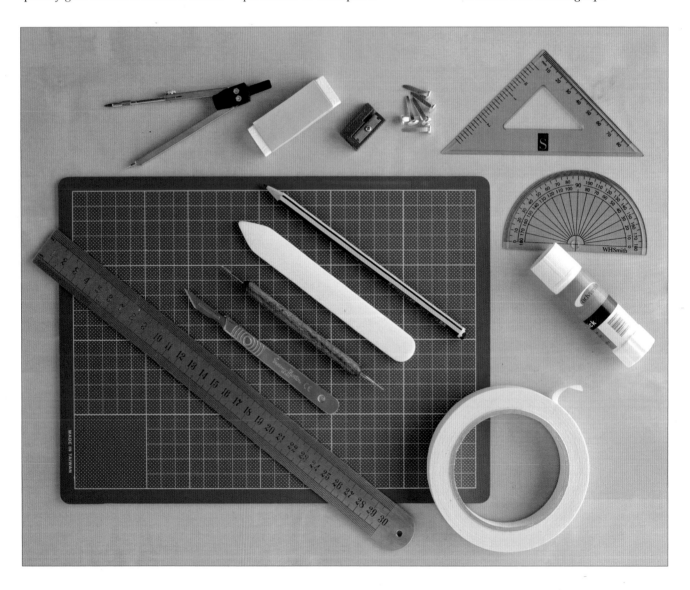

▲ *A compass cutter is ideal for cutting circles, and provides a neater result than a scalpel.*

STEEL RULER

A must for preserving the fingers and cutting neat lines. A 30cm/12in ruler is generally the most useful, but if you are cutting large sheets of card and paper, a 60cm/24in ruler may also come in handy.

PENCIL, SHARPENER & ERASER

A sharp HB-grade pencil is ideal for marking up your designs and is easily erased. A propelling pencil with a disposable lead is also good to use as the point is very fine. A pencil sharpener is essential and a good eraser or putty rubber, which leaves no marks on the paper, is invaluable.

EMBOSSING TOOL

These are tools with wooden or plastic handles and a metal rounded length on one or both ends. They are used to indent paper and card, and are essential to create sharp folds. They can be found easily in any good stationers or craft shop.

BONE FOLDER

These are usually white plastic, although they used to be made of bone. They create neat folds in paper, with a much sharper result than a fingernail. The edge of a pencil, pen or scissors will do almost as well.

PROTRACTOR, COMPASS & SET SQUARE

These are the most technical pieces of equipment required for making pop-ups, and are essential additions to your kit. Measuring precise angles is very important to make sure that your pop-ups fold correctly. A compass ensures that neat, uniform circles of any size can be achieved easily.

COMPASS CUTTER

This strange-looking instrument eliminates the use of the pencil, compass and scalpel when cutting circles. Simply set the measurement to the required radius and place the point on the paper or card to be cut. Swivelling the cutter in a circle while applying light pressure will cut a perfect circle (with a little practice). This is something that is very difficult to achieve with a scalpel.

GLUE

A stick of glue is neat and handy to use and is therefore recommended for most of the projects in this book. There will be times when you need to use a stronger glue such as PVA, which has the added benefit of being peelable – making it less likely to cause damage to paper if you make mistakes. Stronger all-purpose adhesives are best for permanent bonding but can sometimes be very messy to use.

▼ *Felt-tipped pens are invaluable for colouring your designs.*

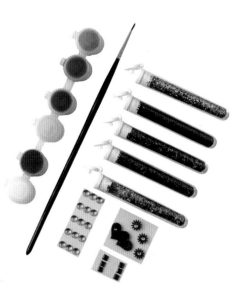

▲ *Paint, glitter and stickers can all be used to add decorative elements to your pop-ups.*

LOW-TACK MASKING TAPE

This is invaluable for making rough models, practice runs, and initial positioning on final projects before you commit to gluing.

DECORATING PAPER AND CARD

Many of the projects in this book involve applying decoration to your designs. This is where it pays to make 'dummies', so that you don't create a complicated design and find it doesn't pop up properly.

A scanner and printer are useful tools, as printing on to a thin card will provide a result that is firm enough for use and has a beautifully smooth surface. There is also the added benefit that you can make as many identical pop-ups as you want without having to re-do the artwork – this is especially useful for creating greetings cards or invitations. In some cases the printer ink may need to be fixed with an art fixative spray to prevent it from smudging.

Use any medium you are comfortable with to decorate card and paper – coloured pencils, felt-tipped pens, paint and glitter give a fabulous finished result.

Techniques and troubleshooting

The information given below should equip you with the basic skills that you need to start making pop-ups. These simple techniques form the basis of many of the projects in this book.

MAKING ROUGHS

A brilliant pop-up has often been through many rough stages with lots of adjustments, resulting in a snowstorm of discarded paper, so always start by creating a rough model first. This not only helps to make sure it works before you start the hard work of decorating, but also helps determine exactly which parts of your design need colour.

MAKING A BACKING SHEET

1 Cut a piece of card or mounting board the same size as your page.

2 Indent a spine fold in card, scoring first if you are using mounting board.

3 Reinforce the inside of the sheet with masking tape if necessary. Attach your completed project to the backing sheet, making sure you have not glued any moving parts.

MAKING TEMPLATES

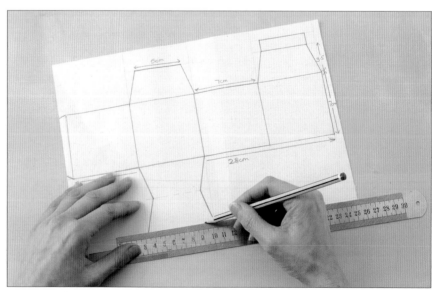

Draw all parts of the design accurately, marking all cut- and fold-lines and any tab positions needed on the page. Use masking tape to fix the tabs, to test positioning before you glue them permanently.

MAKING TABS

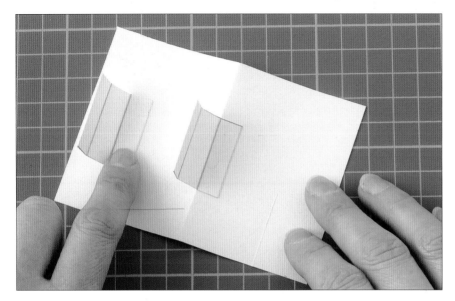

These are crucial for holding everything into place. They need to be large enough to hold the piece but not so big as to get in the way of the design. You can either incorporate them into your pop-up when you are designing it or add them later. In modern pop-up books, tabs are hardly visible, because they have been cleverly disguised within the artwork and cut to complement the design. Another method is to cut slits in the page and slip the tabs underneath to glue.

MAKING A TAB SHEET

This is not an essential, but it can be very useful to have on hand. It is a marked-up sheet with pre-folded lines from which you can easily cut sections to use as ready-folded tabs. The most useful size tabs are 2cm/¾in, so a fold at 1cm/⅜in, 3cm/1³⁄₁₆in and 4cm/1½in from the top of a page would give you a row of 2cm/¾in tabs with 1cm/⅜in fixings at the top and bottom – simply cut a section the width you need for your pop-up piece.

FOLDING TIPS

▲ Creasing by hand is only suitable for thin paper.

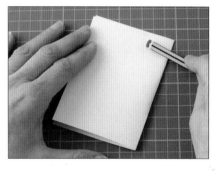

▲ The edge of a pencil can be used to create sharp creases on thin paper.

▲ The handle of a pair of scissors can be used to create neat creases on card.

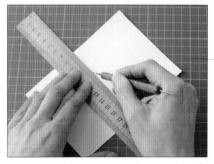

▲ For thicker paper it is best to indent creases before folding. This will result in a neater edge.

CUTTING TIPS

1 Mark the shape that you want to cut on to tracing paper.

2 Transfer to the card or paper you are using for your final design.

3 Mark any lines that are to be cut in bold using a pencil.

4 Softly mark any lines that are to be indented with a pencil; this prevents confusion when you are cutting.

5 Use a metal ruler and a craft knife to make any cuts, following the bold pencil lines marked in step 3.

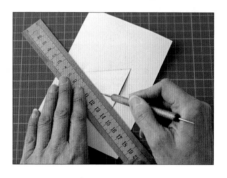

6 Use an embossing tool and metal ruler to indent the lines marked in step 4.

7 Gently push the pop-up through from the back of the card.

8 Use a bone folder to create sharp creases along your indented lines.

TESTING THE POP-UP

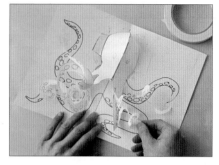

1 Use low-tack masking tape to temporarily affix your pop-up pieces.

2 Experiment with positioning by folding the page before affixing.

3 If you are happy with the position of the mechanism, carefully detach the masking tape from the pop-up.

4 Use glue to stick pieces of the mechanism to their base.

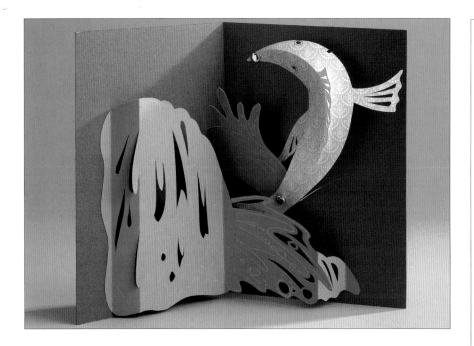

TROUBLESHOOTING

The pop is crooked and not folding correctly – An angle is wrong and the tabs aren't symmetrical. Open the page flat, unstick one tab and attach masking tape to it, then close the page. Providing your angle is not too far out you should be able to open the page with the pop correctly aligned.

The pop is too large to fit in the page – This may mean that the angle of your pop-up is incorrect. If not you will have to reduce the size of your design, or use a larger page as the base for the design.

▲ *Intricate designs require careful cutting and measuring for successful results.*

The pop won't stay flat in the page – If it is not an incorrect angle (see above) the card may be too thick or it is not creased sufficiently.

The pop is stuck and the page won't open – Check that there is no glue sticking the mechanism to the page. If there is it should be possible to carefully part the pages with the sharp edge of a craft knife.

▼ *Practice and patience will allow you to create impressive designs.*

TERMINOLOGY

Most people have come across Origami terms so some of these should be quite familiar:

Valley fold – a downward fold away from you.
Mountain fold – an upwards fold towards you.
Reverse fold – folding once then adding another fold to face the other way.
Concertina fold – a series of alternating mountain and valley folds along the page.
Spine – the fold down the centre of the page.
Draw cut lines – draw darker lines marking where to cut.
Draw fold lines – draw very light lines marking where you will fold.
Base line – the lowest line of your shape.
Tabs – these can be drawn into the pop design or added on later, enabling the piece to be glued to the page.
Indenting – indenting a line with the embossing tool for folding.
Creasing – to firmly fold the indented line.
Scoring – to partly cut through the card which is too thick to fold. This is only needed on very sturdy pop-ups.
Templates – a copy of your design that you can easily reproduce, instead of making from scratch every time. These can be scanned on a computer or photocopied, but tracing on to tracing paper works just as well.
Backing sheet – a folded sheet of thick card or mounting board the same size as your page. Used to back the pop-up and strengthen it, it also disguises tabs that are glued to the reverse of a pop-up.

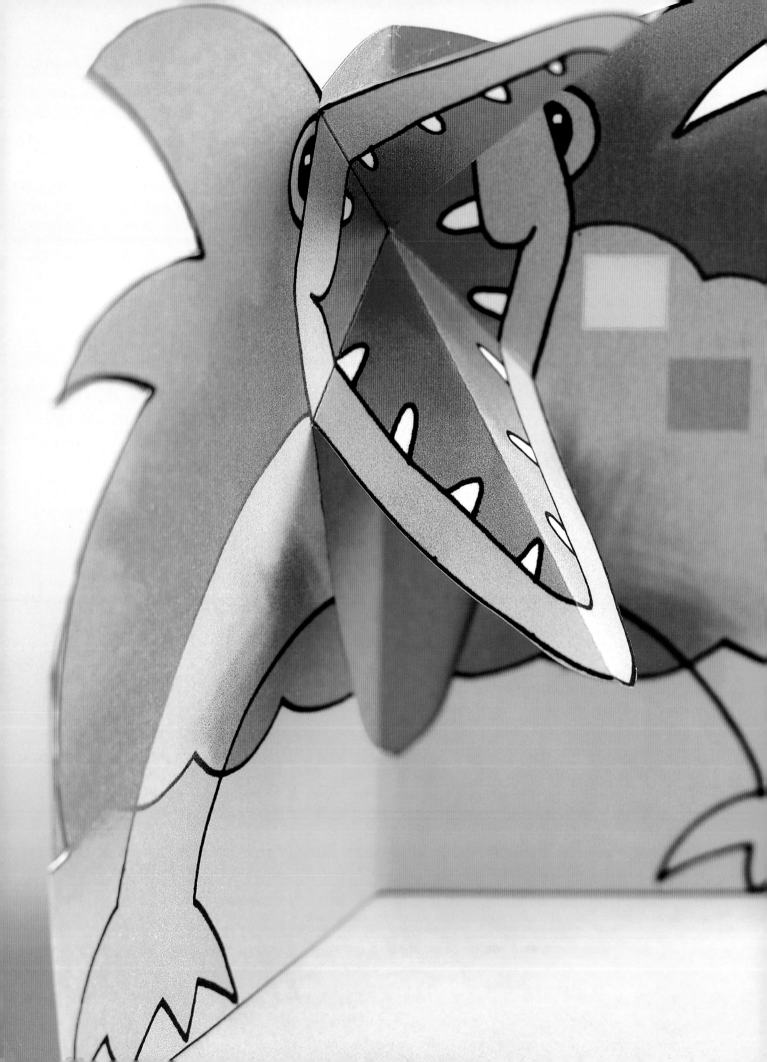

Simple folds and cards

Excitingly dynamic pop-ups don't have to be difficult to make, and these projects explore the simple techniques that will allow you to begin creating your own pop-up cards. The techniques that are taught in this section, such as the basic folds, form the basis of many more complicated pop-up designs, so it is worth taking the time to master them.

This chapter features beautiful designs for a festive pop-up angel and Christmas tree cards; entertaining animal pop-ups including a crocodile, a wolf and a spider; and simple and elegant designs such as an autumnal leaf and an impressive Mayan pyramid, among many others.

Basic V/A fold

This basic fold is the backbone of many intricate pop-ups, creating fun and exciting movements and adding great depth to a design. Depending on which orientation you use this simple form produces a V or an A shape and a sideways movement sweeping upwards or downwards.

MATERIALS AND EQUIPMENT
A6 paper
bone folder
cutting mat
metal ruler
craft knife
embossing tool

1 Fold the sheet of paper in half widthways.

TIP
Always keep the cut less than half the width of the folded sheet so that the pop-up does not extend beyond the edges of the closed card.

2 Using a metal ruler and a craft knife, make a horizontal cut about two-thirds of the way down the card, cutting from the fold to less than halfway across.

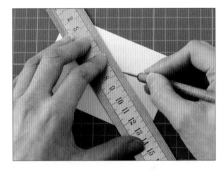

3 Using the ruler and an embossing tool, indent a line from one-third of the way along the fold down to the end of the cut.

4 Fold along the indented line, unfold, open out the sheet and push the triangle in from the back, re-creasing both diagonal folds inwards so that it sits inside the closed card.

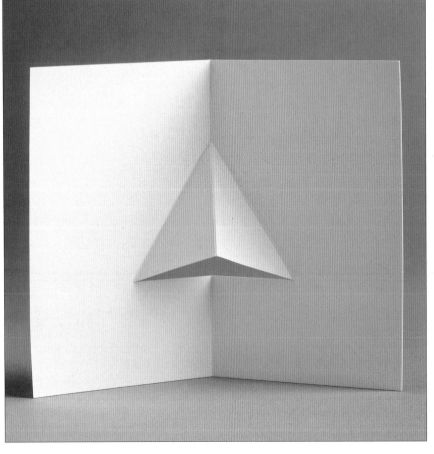

Angel

This simple pop-up using the V/A fold would make a great greetings card for Christmas. Add colour and glitter if you like, plus a gold backing sheet for extra seasonal sparkle.

MATERIALS AND EQUIPMENT
A5 thick paper or thin card (stock)
bone folder
pencil
cutting mat
metal ruler
embossing tool
craft knife
A5 tracing or decorative paper
glue

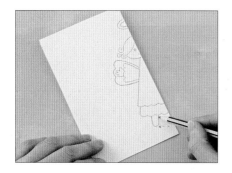

1 Fold the paper in half widthways. On the outside, along the fold, lightly draw one half of an angel: a head, a halo and a triangular dress. Draw a wing attached to the body, with an arm and sleeve inside the wing.

2 Using a ruler and an embossing tool, indent the diagonal line from the neck to the hem of the dress. Indent short vertical lines at the outer edges of the head and halo.

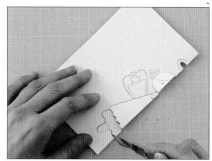

3 Cutting through both layers, cut around the halo up to the indented line (cut out the middle of the halo completely) and do the same with the head. Cut out the base of the dress, up to the diagonal fold.

4 Carefully cut around the wing, but do not cut the line between the wing and the body. Then, cut around the sleeve and hand and remove the wing section.

5 Crease all the indented lines, then open the card slightly. Push all the shapes through and close the card to flatten the folds.

6 Open the card and fold the arms in towards the body to give a 3D look. The angel's hair and features can be drawn on or cut out, and glitter added. Glue the card to a backing sheet of tracing paper or decorative paper.

V/A fold with inverse

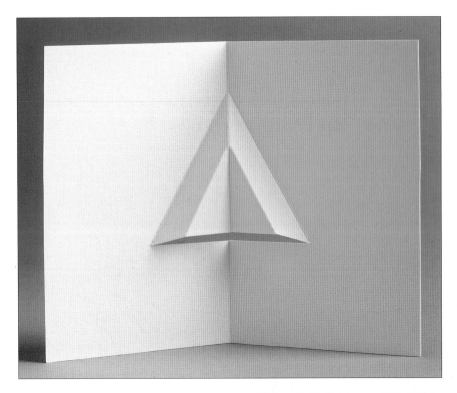

This technique is a variation on the basic V/A fold, adding interest to the fold and also changing the movement created, from a sideways swoop to an up-and-down movement.

MATERIALS AND EQUIPMENT
A6 paper
bone folder
cutting mat
metal ruler
craft knife
embossing tool

1 Fold the sheet of paper in half widthways.

2 Using a metal ruler and a craft knife, make a horizontal cut about two-thirds of the way down the card, cutting from the fold to less than halfway across.

TIP
An embossing tool is very useful when making pop-ups, as it will allow you to neatly indent folds in card and paper without the risk of accidental cutting. If you do not have access to one, an empty ballpoint pen makes a good alternative.

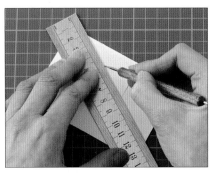

3 Using a ruler and embossing tool (see Tip), indent a line from one-third of the way down the fold to the end of the cut. Inside this line, indent another line parallel to it, making an inner triangle.

4 Carefully fold along both of the indented lines, unfold, open out the sheet and push the triangle in from the back using the longer creases.

5 Reverse-fold the inner triangle created by the shorter creases and gently close the card to test the pop-up.

Dog

This project is an easy example of how to use the inverse V/A fold effectively: the larger fold makes the snout of the dog and the smaller one makes the nose. Once you have made a small-scale rough model this is a fun design to try on a larger scale.

MATERIALS AND EQUIPMENT
2 sheets of A5 paper
bone folder
pencil
set square
felt-tipped pens
cutting mat
metal ruler
craft knife
embossing tool
A5 coloured card (stock)
glue

1 Fold the paper in half widthways, and unfold. Lightly draw guidelines for two A folds of 90°, one inside the other.

2 Draw the dog's face, using the guidelines to position the nose, and colour in the face.

3 Indent the fold lines and cut out the dog's head. Valley-fold the snout and inverse-fold the nose section.

4 Fold the card in half widthways and unfold. Lay the dog's head on the fold. Mark the position of the valley fold and draw around the bottom of the head, adding a chin.

5 Cut out the middle section, following the line of the A fold at the top and the chin at the bottom, then glue the head to the card.

6 Draw the inside of the dog's open mouth on to the second sheet of paper and attach as a backing sheet. Fold shut to test the pop-up.

V/A fold, varying the cut line

This variation on the simple V/A fold keeps the same angle of crease but varies the cut line so that it is no longer symmetrical.

MATERIALS AND EQUIPMENT
A6 paper
bone folder
pair of compasses
cutting mat
metal ruler
craft knife
embossing tool

TIP
When creasing lines of differing lengths it is always easier to crease the longer one first.

1 Fold the sheet of paper in half widthways. With the paper still folded, use a compass point to mark the top of the A fold along the spine, near to the top of the page. Then, mark the outermost point of the triangle, piercing both layers.

2 Open out the sheet, and on the front, draw faint guidelines from the fold through the outer marked points of the triangle.

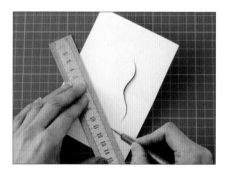

3 Cut a diagonal wavy line from one guideline to the other. (You can draw this first if you like.) Use an embossing tool to indent the fold lines, which will be different lengths, and re-fold the sheet.

4 Crease the indent lines and push the triangle through to the inside from the back. Carefully fold the paper to test the pop-up.

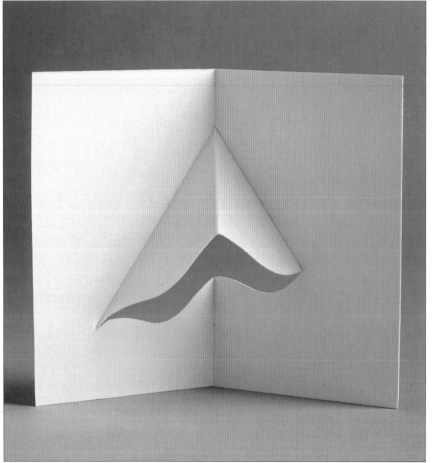

Cat on the wall

This cat is framed by the harvest moon. The design is very easy to do, but remember not to make a central fold for the spine at the outset.

MATERIALS AND EQUIPMENT
A5 coloured card (stock)
metal ruler
pencil
A5 tracing paper
pair of compasses
felt-tipped pens
cutting mat
craft knife
embossing tool
glue
brick-effect decorative paper

1 With the coloured card in landscape mode, do not fold but mark the central spine and draw a small A fold to make the body of the cat.

2 Draw the design on tracing paper: place the body centrally, with the tail coming from one side to swish across. The head should be above the A fold and the background will be cut in a semicircle for the moon.

3 Transfer the design on to the card and colour in the cat with felt-tipped pens.

4 Cut around the base of the cat, including the tail, up to the marked A-fold lines on each side.

5 Indent the fold lines and fold the card in half, pushing the cat's body inwards, so that the tail doesn't fold but moves into place.

6 Cut around the outside of the design and glue on the brick-effect paper.

V/A fold, varying the fold angle

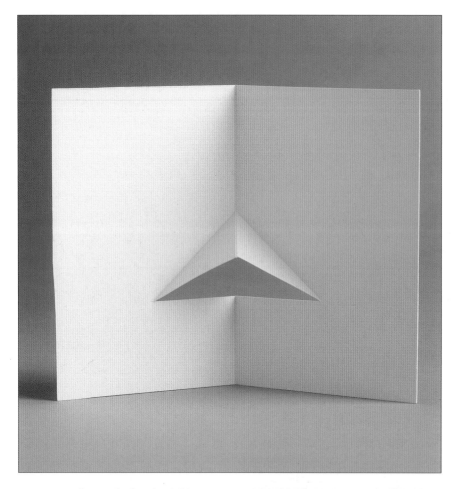

Using a wider angle for the fold creates a bigger movement as the pop-up is opened.

MATERIALS AND EQUIPMENT
A6 paper
bone folder
cutting mat
metal ruler
craft knife
embossing tool

TIP
A more acute angle increases the height of the pop-up inside the card; to allow for this, keep A folds nearer to the bottom of the sheet and V folds nearer to the top.

1 Fold the sheet of paper in half widthways and make a horizontal cut from the fold as in the basic A/V fold technique. This should be about three-quarters of the way down the card and two-thirds of the way across.

2 Using a ruler and an embossing tool, indent a fold line from about halfway down the spine to the outer edge of the cut line.

3 Fold firmly along the indent line then unfold.

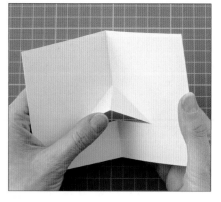

4 Open out the sheet and push the pop-up through from the back, re-creasing the folds inwards so that the pop-up sits inside the fold when closed.

Wide-mouthed frog

This project uses a wide-angled A fold to great effect. Use green decorative paper to make the frog and blue card for the pond.

MATERIALS AND EQUIPMENT
A5 paper in green and pink
bone folder
pencil
cutting mat
metal ruler
embossing tool
pair of compasses
craft knife
felt-tipped pens
A5 thin blue card (stock)
glue

1 Fold the green paper in half widthways. Draw a long wavy mouth from the spine two-thirds of the way down the page. Indent a fold line from halfway down the spine to the outer edge of the mouth and mark these points through both layers using a compass point.

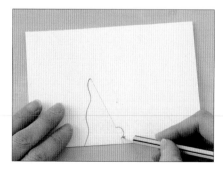

2 To add the eyes, draw a semicircle centrally on the indented line.

3 Cut along the wavy mouth and fold the indented line, using a bone folder to make a sharp crease. Push the head through and re-close the fold.

4 Cut around the sides of the eyes, but leave 5mm/¼in sections, parallel to the indent line, uncut at the top and bottom. Indent and fold.

5 Now push each eye through to the right side and re-crease the folds.

6 Turn to the right side and draw in the eyes. Fold a sheet of blue card in half, cut out the shape of the frog's head and glue it on to the front. Glue a sheet of pink paper to the back for the inside of the mouth.

Beak fold

This name of this basic fold is self-explanatory. The angle can vary depending on how far you want the pop-up to lift, but the cut is deep, creating a lovely, long shape. Add a coloured backing sheet to complete the look of a beak.

MATERIALS AND EQUIPMENT
A6 paper
bone folder
cutting mat
metal ruler
craft knife

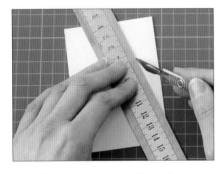

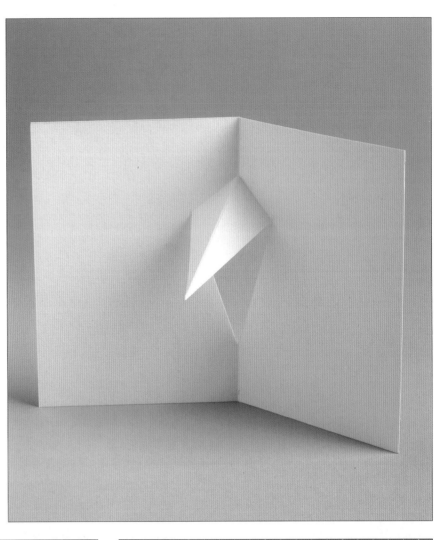

1 Fold the paper in half widthways. Make a long diagonal cut, starting a little above halfway down and about 2cm/¾in in from the fold, to meet the fold near the bottom.

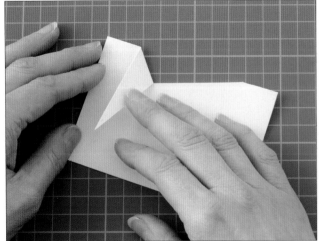

2 To make sure the pop-up piece doesn't stick out of the card when closed, fold it without indenting first, deciding on the angle as you fold.

3 Unfold, open out the paper and push the pop-up through from the back, checking as you re-fold that the beak is sitting properly inside the card.

Leaf

The beak fold is usually cut and coloured to make bird designs, but in this project the basic shape is used with additional cuts to make a delicate leaf design that would be perfect for an autumnal greetings card.

MATERIALS AND EQUIPMENT
A5 paper in two colours
bone folder
metal ruler
pencil
cutting mat
craft knife
embossing tool
glue

1 Fold one sheet of paper in half widthways. Draw a diagonal line from near the top of the fold, and a curving serrated leaf outline from it back to the fold. Use a craft knife to cut along the serrated outline.

2 Indent and fold the diagonal line. Open the card and push in the pop-up, re-creasing the folds inwards to ensure a good fit.

3 Open out the paper, and on the back of the leaf, carefully cut vein patterns (draw these first if necessary), taking care to leave a wide margin around the edge.

4 Re-fold the leaf into the card and add a coloured backing sheet.

> **TIP**
> Thicker leaf veins will ensure a more solid and long-lasting pop-up.

Off-centre V/A fold

This looks a bit wonky but creates an interesting sideways movement when opened. The technique is a bit trickier than the basic fold as it involves some measuring of angles, so you will need to use a protractor.

MATERIALS AND EQUIPMENT
A6 paper
metal ruler
pencil
protractor
cutting mat
craft knife
embossing tool

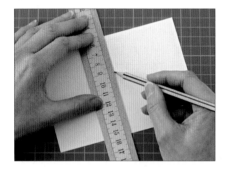

1 Arrange the paper in landscape mode, but don't fold it. Carefully measure the page and lightly mark the centre line using a pencil and a metal ruler.

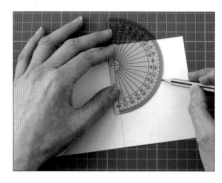

2 From a starting point a quarter of the way down, draw two lines at different angles to the centre line, say 25° on one side and 65° on the other.

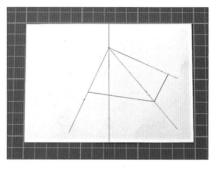

3 From the same point draw a third line between the first two, taking the smaller measurement used in step 2 from the line drawn at the bigger angle: in this case measure 25° from the line drawn at 65°.

4 Mark out and cut the line at the base of your shape.

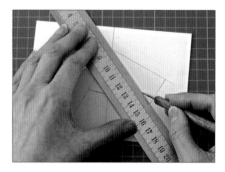

5 Indent all three fold lines and also the central fold line above and below the shape.

6 Crease each fold line, and ease the shape into place as you close the fold.

TIP
To avoid measuring angles, indent the two outer edges of the shape and cut the base line by eye. As you close the central fold, keeping the indented lines folded, the third crease will automatically form.

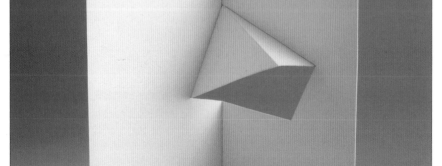

Wolf

This design uses the off-centre technique to produce a sideways movement, which is ideal for a wolf or any other sly-looking long-snouted creature.

MATERIALS AND EQUIPMENT
A5 tracing paper
metal ruler
pencil
protractor
A5 white paper
felt-tipped pens
cutting mat
pair of compasses
craft knife
embossing tool
bone folder
A5 coloured card (stock)
glue

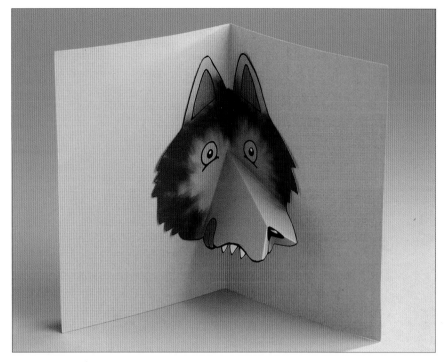

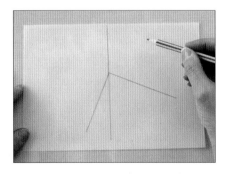

1 Arrange a sheet of tracing paper with the long side towards you, and draw the centre line. From a point about halfway down, draw the two outer lines for the pop-up at 25° and 65°. Draw a third line between the two at an angle of 25° from the wide-angle line.

> **TIP**
> When gluing your design to a backing sheet, make sure that you are not affixing any parts that need to move freely; in this case it is important not to glue the snout.

2 Lay another sheet of tracing paper over the first and draw your design on it, using the angled lines as a guide to the position of the wolf's snout.

3 Transfer the design to white paper and colour it in.

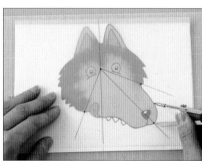

4 Place the tracing paper with the guidelines over the design and mark the ends of the fold lines.

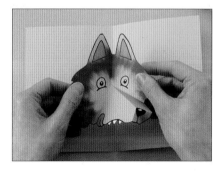

5 Cut around the head. Indent each fold line, adding a small inverse fold around the nose. Attach the head to a folded backing sheet.

V/A folds with extensions

This sounds more complicated than it is – it means simply extending the pop-up forward by cutting around some sections and not folding them, so that they stick out further.

MATERIALS AND EQUIPMENT
A6 paper
metal ruler
pencil
protractor
cutting mat
craft knife
embossing tool

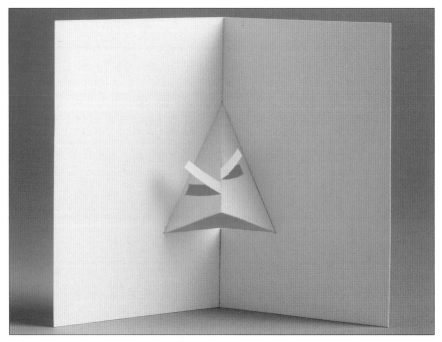

1 Turn a sheet of A6 paper with the long edge towards you, and lightly draw a line down the centre.

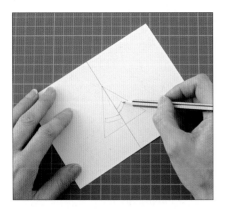

2 Draw a symmetrical triangle centred on the line. Draw two curved extension shapes from the centre line, keeping them within the triangle.

3 Cut the base line and all around the extensions (leaving them uncut at the centre).

4 Indent the central fold above and below the triangle and the two outer fold lines. Indent between the extensions, carefully avoiding the extensions themselves.

5 Pick up the paper and crease each fold line individually, starting with the outer creases of the triangle. As the shape starts to pop out, the extensions should naturally stick out, allowing you to make the central fold without creasing them.

TIP
When drawing multiple extensions, make sure there is space between each one on the centre line for support, otherwise the pop-up will fall apart.

Christmas tree

This is a wonderful Christmas card design that uses the V/A fold with extensions tehnique. A seasonal message can be added on the outside.

MATERIALS AND EQUIPMENT
A4 red paper
bone folder
A5 green card (stock)
metal ruler
pencil
protractor
pair of compasses
cutting mat
craft knife
tracing paper
embossing tool
glue
glitter or paint

1 Fold the A4 paper in half, then in half again. Unfold and lay flat.

2 On the back of the green card, mark the centre line and draw two lines 10cm/4in long at 30° to it. Using compasses, draw a curve joining the two diagonals for the base, and further curves at 1cm/⅜in intervals.

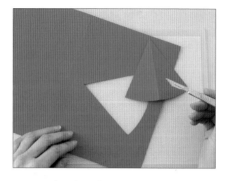

3 Transfer the shape on the card to the centre fold of the lower half of the coloured paper and cut it out.

4 On the card, cut the extensions on the curves, alternating the edge cuts, leaving small gaps between them at the centre. Indent the spine above and below the tree and between the extensions, and the diagonal folds.

5 Pick up the card and crease each diagonal fold. As the shape starts to pop out, allow the extensions to follow, while folding the spine.

6 Glue the tree in place inside the outer sheet, trimming the edges if necessary for a better fit; the smaller the area around the tree, the easier it will be to fold.

V above A fold

These two basic folds work well together, creating a striking effect when the card is opened.

MATERIALS AND EQUIPMENT
A6 paper
bone folder
cutting mat
metal ruler
craft knife
embossing tool

TIP
This makes an ideal gift tag when made in a bright colour.

1 Fold the paper in half widthways. From the fold, cut two horizontal lines of equal length near the top and bottom.

2 Indent two fold lines from the spine to the outer edges of the cut lines; there should be a gap between the top and bottom triangles.

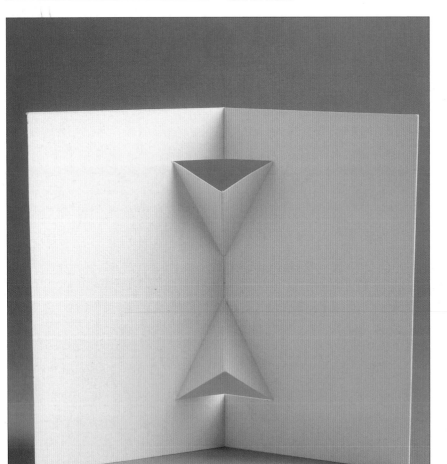

3 Fold along the indented fold lines, unfold, open out the paper and push the pop-ups inwards from the back.

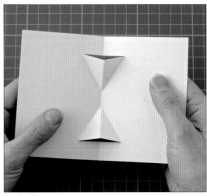

4 Carefully re-crease the folds so that the pop-ups sit properly inside the card when closed.

The hungry croc

V above A folds are ideal for a crocodile's big, opening mouth, but you can apply the idea to any animal or bird by varying the shape of the jaws or beak. Moving the V and A folds further apart will create a different effect.

MATERIALS AND EQUIPMENT
A4 tracing paper
metal ruler
pencil
protractor
A4 white and blue paper
felt-tipped pens or paints
cutting mat
embossing tool
craft knife
glue

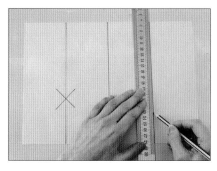

1 With the long side of the tracing paper toward you, draw vertical fold lines to divide it into four equal sections. 7.5cm/3in up from the bottom of the first fold line, draw a cross with lines at 45° to the vertical.

> **TIP**
> As these V and A folds are touching (you could call it an X fold), be sure not to make the angles larger than 45°, otherwise when the card is closed, the folded edges will not touch neatly together but will overlap, and it may make it difficult to shut.

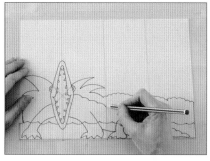

2 Place a second sheet of tracing paper over the first and draw the crocodile – with ferocious, wide-open jaws positioned directly over the cross marked in step 1 – and a watery background.

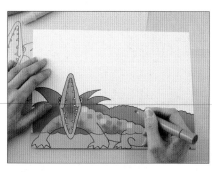

3 Transfer the drawing to white paper with the second sheet of tracing paper and colour the design in using felt-tipped pens.

4 Indent the lines of the cross and the vertical folds, using the lines drawn in step 1 to mark the fold positions.

5 Cut around the background shape and the top and bottom jaws, leaving the middle section of the cross uncut. Indent the cross and vertical fold lines, and push the jaws forward. Use the tracing design to cut out a backing sheet and glue in place.

A above V fold

With the position of the two basic folds reversed, they can be used to make a closing mouth or beak, which could be even more frightening than the crocodile's gaping jaws!

MATERIALS AND EQUIPMENT
A6 paper
bone folder
cutting mat
metal ruler
craft knife
embossing tool

1 Fold the paper in half widthways. Cut one horizontal line from the centre of the fold.

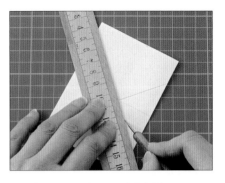

2 Indent two diagonal fold lines from the cut line to the fold, above and below the centre.

3 Fold the indent lines, unfold, open out the paper and push in the pop-up.

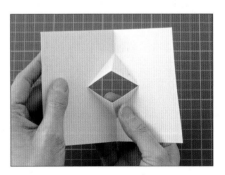

4 Re-crease the folds so that the pop-up sits nicely inside when closed.

TIP
Ensure that the horizontal cut line is not wider than halfway across the page or the pop may be too large and protrude when the page is closed. For neatness use a bone folder to get a tidy crease edge.

Chameleon

The A above V fold produces a great closing movement suitable for many different animals – shown here is a chameleon. This will need separate sheets for the background colour and for the inside of the mouth.

MATERIALS AND EQUIPMENT
A5 green, patterned and pink paper
bone folder
metal ruler
pencil
cutting mat
embossing tool
craft knife
glue

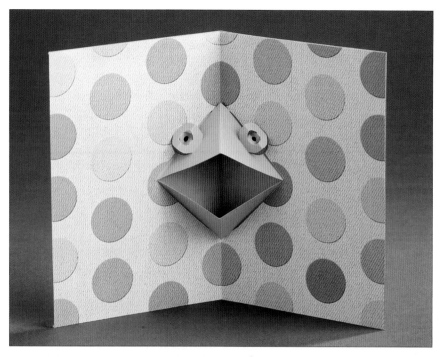

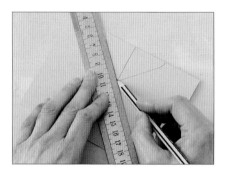

1 Fold the green paper in half widthways. From the fold, mark half a diamond shape, rounding off the lines at the top and bottom, and a horizontal line through the centre. Draw a large circle for the eyes, with the centre along the top diagonal.

3 Push through to the front. On the back, cut around the eyes, leaving the sections parallel to the head uncut.

5 Re-fold the sheet, place on a folded background sheet and trace the cut-out shape on to it.

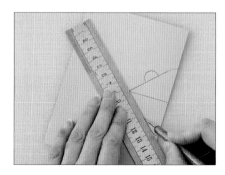

2 Indent the diagonal fold lines, up to the curved lines at top and bottom, then cut the curved lines and the centre line for the mouth.

4 Indent the eyes along the fold lines and push to the front. For added effect you can cut a smaller circle inside each eye and reverse fold it.

6 Cut the shape out of the background sheet and glue it in place over the chameleon. Add a pink backing sheet to finish.

Adding on V/A folds

The techniques shown so far have involved cutting into the paper or card to create the pop-up, giving an idea of some of the movements that can be achieved. When you add pieces you can make far more complex shapes, giving you more scope and making the pop-ups bigger and more effective.

MATERIALS AND EQUIPMENT
A6 and A7 paper
cutting mat
bone folder
metal ruler
embossing tool
craft knife
masking tape
glue

1 Start with a sheet of A6 paper folded widthways in the centre and opened out. Take a second sheet half this size and fold it in half, using a bone folder to give a sharp crease.

2 On the smaller sheet, indent a line at right angles to the spine fold and about 1cm/⅜in from the edge.

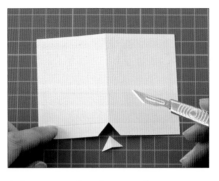

3 Open out the sheet and cut a small V in the centre of the indented section, creating two separate tabs.

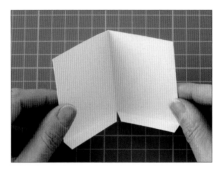

4 Fold in the two tabs along the indent lines and fold the spine slightly. Each tab must be attached to the base page at an angle of less than 90° from the central spine.

5 Use tape to fix one tab to the base, aligning the spines. Fold the shape on to one side of the page, attach tape to the other tab and close the page.

6 This should ensure a perfect fit, but test by opening and closing, and adjust the position if necessary before attaching permanently with glue.

Winter scene

You can create an entire three-dimensional landscape adding V/A folds as the vertical elements, and the base page as the ground. It is a good idea to make a rough version first, to make sure all the layers fit inside and to shape the base around the layers.

MATERIALS AND EQUIPMENT
A5 and A4 paper
bone folder
metal ruler
pencil
protractor
felt-tipped pens
glue
glitter
cutting mat
embossing tool
craft knife
masking tape

1 Fold an A5 sheet in half widthways and open out for the "ground". Mark the positions for the scenery – in this case there will be three layers, each at an angle of 75° from the spine.

TIP
V folds need to be placed higher up on the page and A folds further down in order to fit when folded. If the base shape isn't rectangular, do a trial version to ensure all the folded layers are contained within it.

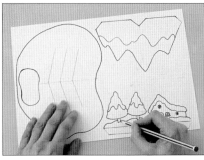

2 Draw all the layers on a larger sheet. As a rough guide, each should be no more than half the size of the base, and each will need a central fold and 1cm/⅜in tabs along the bottom. The base shape shown here has already been tested for size (see tip).

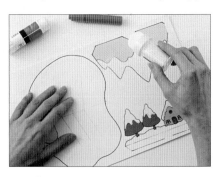

3 Colour the layers, adding snowy white glitter for a wintry feel.

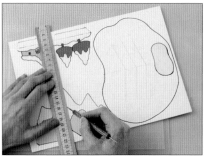

4 Indent all the folds and cut out the layers and the base.

5 Attach the back layer: secure one tab to the page at the marked position, add tape or glue to the other tab and close the page on to it: this helps to get the layer central. Attach the final two layers in the same way.

Adding on V/A fold with angle change

Changing the angle of the pop-up and the position of the tabs will exaggerate the upward or downward movement of the pop-up so that it will literally pop out of the page. Experiment with different angles for a variety of effects.

MATERIALS AND EQUIPMENT
A6 and A7 paper
bone folder
metal ruler
protractor
pencil
cutting mat
embossing tool
glue

TIP
To get the same angle on each side of the pop-up, fold it in half, measure and draw the line on one side, then prick the end point through with a compass point to get a precise point to draw to on the other side.

1 Fold a sheet of A6 paper in half widthways and open out. Mark tab positions at 35° from the central fold.

2 Take an A7 sheet and fold it in half. From the base of the spine, draw two lines at 55°. These two angles together will keep the pop-up within the closed base.

3 Indent and crease the angled lines to make the tabs (in a finished piece you can cut the tabs down to make them smaller).

4 Attach one tab at the marked position, fold the pop-up down and glue the other tab, then close the page over it.

Spider

This is a simple project for Halloween to delight any child, as the creepy creature really does seem to jump right out of the page. In this design the base of the V fold is cut away, making it harder to centre the pop-up, but by sticking one tab first, adding tape to the other tab then closing the fold you should get a good result.

MATERIALS AND EQUIPMENT
protractor
pencil
metal ruler
A4 paper
felt-tipped pens
cutting mat
craft knife
coloured paper scraps
glue
21cm/8⅜in square of
    coloured paper
bone folder
glitter
embossing tool
masking tape

1 On A4 paper, draw a central vertical line and two diagonal lines at an angle of 70°. Draw the spider, 11cm/4⅜in high and 20cm/8in wide, mostly above the angled lines but with the feet overlapping to form the tabs. (Make sure the lines are still visible on the legs.) Colour the spider in using felt-tipped pens.

2 Cut out the spider, leaving a wide enough area of the legs and feet uncut to support the body easily. Add other features cut from coloured paper.

3 Fold the square paper in half and open out. From the centre, draw two lines at 45° on either side of the spine for the tab positions. Decorate with a glittery web, making sure the guidelines are still visible.

4 Indent the marked lines at the base of the spider's legs and fold to make the tabs.

5 Place the spider centrally on the decorated base, taping the feet to the 45° angled guidelines. Test the pop-up by closing it carefully – the feet may need to be re-aligned before they are glued permanently in place.

V with multiple inverse folds

This technique creates a very intricate-looking pop-up, but in fact it is quite simple to do. Make sure the folds are exactly parallel and evenly spaced for the best effect.

MATERIALS AND EQUIPMENT
A5 paper
bone folder
metal ruler
pencil
cutting mat
embossing tool
craft knife

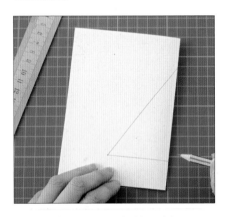

1 Fold the paper in half widthways and draw a triangle from the spine fold, 9cm/3½in high and 6cm/2¼in across on both sides of the spine.

2 Mark five points at 1.5cm/⁹⁄₁₆in intervals down the spine fold and five points at 1cm/³⁄₈in intervals on each horizontal, then join the points with five parallel lines.

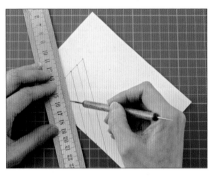

3 Indent all the diagonal fold lines with an embossing tool and ruler.

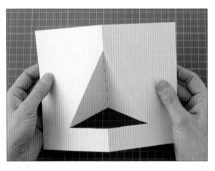

4 Cut the base line of the triangle, open out the paper and fold the largest triangle in.

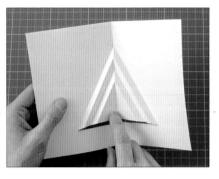

5 Inverse-fold the next triangle and repeat, alternating the folds, until you reach the centre.

TIP
The smaller V folds do not all need to be drawn in at the outset. For a less uniform look, begin by drawing, cutting and folding the largest triangle, then fold the smaller ones freehand.

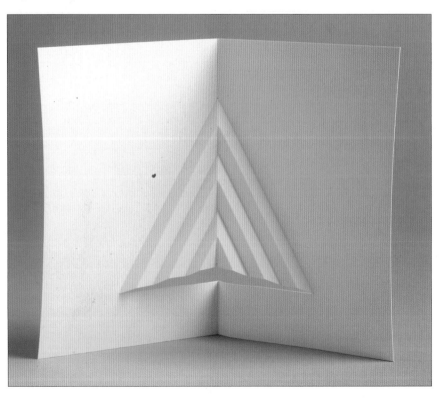

Ice cream sundae

This is a tasty-looking example of multiple inverse folds, and also showcases the use of different coloured papers and glitter.

MATERIALS AND EQUIPMENT
A4 coloured paper or thin card (stock)
bone folder
metal ruler
pencil
protractor
pair of compasses
tracing paper
cutting mat
craft knife
embossing tool
glue
glitter

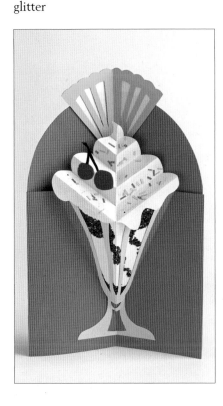

TIP
This is designed as a card, but the two sides could be glued flat, and a message added to the reverse, for a sturdier result.

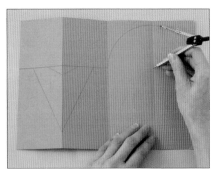

1 Fold an A4 sheet in half and in half again, then open out. On the left half, draw a large V beginning 2cm/¾in from the bottom that is 13.5cm/5⁵⁄₁₆in high and 10cm/4in wide. Draw a smaller V beginning 11.5cm/4½in up from the bottom, with angles of 60° to the spine. Draw a semicircle at the top of the right half of the page for the background.

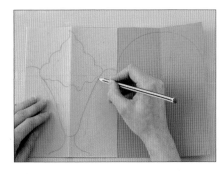

2 Draw the design for the ice cream on tracing paper over these guidelines: the base of the glass should reach the point of the large V and the sides should follow the V folds; the ice cream should finish below the top of the V fold – this section will become a tab. Cut along the top of the background sheet.

3 Transfer the design of the ice cream top to a sheet of white paper marked with a spine fold. Mark the fold lines at 60° either side of spine, 1.5cm/⁹⁄₁₆in apart. Transfer the outline of the glass on to pale blue paper and cut out.

4 Cut around the ice cream and indent the V-fold lines with an embossing tool.

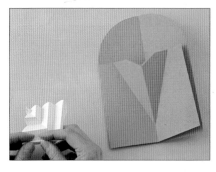

5 Fold the indented lines as follows: on the base the spine is a valley fold, the glass is a mountain fold so that it sticks out, and the small V tab is a valley fold; on the ice cream the folds alternate, starting with a mountain fold to hang over the glass. Decorate the glass with glitter.

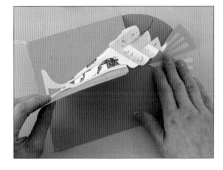

6 Assemble the ice cream and attach to the folded V tab; decorate the background page with a wafer made from yellow card. Decorate the sundae to your taste, adding paper cherries to one of the folds.

A folds on A folds

In this technique the A folds that have previously been described are layered for greater impact. As this pop-up has multiple gaps it may look better, and be more structurally sound, with an additional backing sheet.

MATERIALS AND EQUIPMENT
A5 paper
bone folder
cutting mat
metal ruler
craft knife
embossing tool

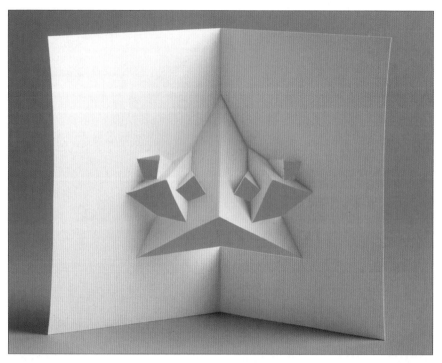

1 Fold the paper in half widthways. With the paper still folded, cut a horizontal line from the spine about three-quarters of the way down, keeping the cut less than two-thirds of the width of the folded sheet. Indent diagonal lines from a quarter of the way down the spine to each end of the horizontal cut line.

2 Fold along the indent line, unfold, open out the page and push the pop-up in from the back.

3 Keeping the triangle folded, cut a base line for a smaller triangle one-third of the way along each diagonal, then open the paper out, indent and crease on both sides.

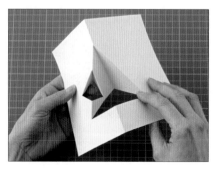

4 Push the two smaller As through on either side of the large A.

5 Re-fold with all the A folds in place and cut another line across each diagonal of the two smaller A folds. As these are now quite small it is easier to fold and push them through without indenting first.

TIP
The smaller the triangles get the more difficult they are to fold. To get neat creases, use any tool that will fit, from a bone folder or embossing tool to the handle of the scalpel or the edge of a pencil.

Peacock

This card is not much harder than the basic technique, but dramatic results can be achieved by adding decoration to the folds.

MATERIALS AND EQUIPMENT
A6 yellow paper
bone folder
metal ruler
pencil
protractor
pair of compasses
cutting mat
embossing tool
craft knife
brown, blue and orange paper
glue
blue glitter

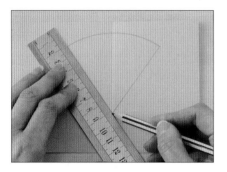

1 Fold a sheet of paper in half widthways and open out. Draw a V fold starting 2cm/¾in from the bottom, with sides 7cm/2¾in long at 30° to the spine. Use compasses to draw a curve at the top.

2 Indent the diagonal lines, cut the top curve, fold the indent lines then push the triangle through to the front.

3 On the back of the paper draw a smaller version of the triangle along each diagonal line. Indent, cut and fold both small triangles and push them through.

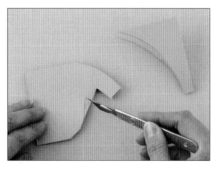

4 With both new triangles folded in, repeat to produce four more triangles within them, making sure they are not too wide to go over the middle section of the largest triangle. Shape the top edge of the sheet into a curve.

5 Assemble 24 feathers from coloured paper and glitter, and glue them on to each triangle.

6 Make an additional V fold from a separate sheet and glue on the body, feet and beak. Draw base tabs, where the feet will stand, at an angle of 70° on each side of the centre fold. Attach one side first, add tape to the other side and close the card to get a good fit, before attaching permanently.

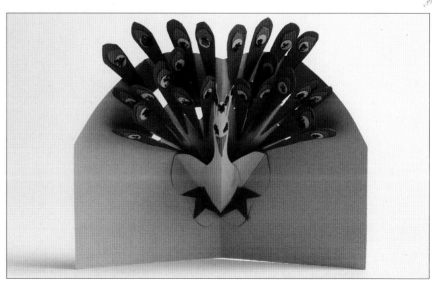

Off-centre basic layer

Along with the V/A fold, the layer fold (also known as a step fold or a parallelogram) is a basic technique that can be used to create single or multiple layers. It is another "backbone" mechanism, producing a straight side-to-side movement as opposed to a swooping movement.

MATERIALS AND EQUIPMENT
A6 paper
metal ruler
pencil
cutting mat
embossing tool
craft knife

1 With the long side of the paper toward you, mark the central spine but do not fold it at this stage.

2 Draw a rectangle off-centre across the centre of the spine: in this example the left side of the rectangle is 2cm/¾in to the left of the spine.

3 Indent the vertical sides of the rectangle and the spine above and below it. Indent the line for the front corner of the rectangle also, 2cm/¾in in from the right side.

TIP
The distance from the left of the rectangle to the spine is the same as the pop-up will stick out over the right-hand page when closed. Ensure the margin to the right of the card is the same as the overlap on the left, plus at least 5cm/2in.

4 Cut along the horizontal lines of the rectangle and crease all the vertical lines.

5 Push the pop-up through to the inside of the fold.

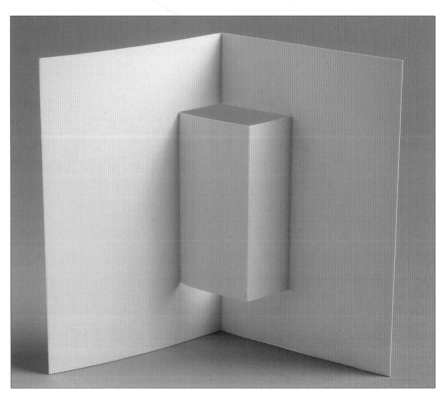

Hole in one

This easy card is great for Father's Day; if your dad isn't a golf fan it could be adapted for any other ball sport. It shows the type of movement you can create with an off-centre fold on a single sheet – later in this book you will see how even more can be achieved by adding another layer.

MATERIALS AND EQUIPMENT
A6 white and green paper
metal ruler
pencil
felt-tipped pens
cutting mat
embossing tool
craft knife
glue

1 With the long edge of the white paper toward you, mark the central spine but do not fold it. Draw a rectangle 7cm/2¾in wide, starting 3cm/1¼in to the left of the spine, and mark a vertical fold line 3cm/1¼in in from the right vertical.

TIP
Regardless of how you choose to position the rectangle, this design will only work with the movement going from right to left. Horizontal slits can be cut in the 'flight path' section of the pop to make it look less solid.

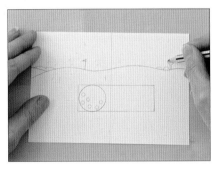

2 Draw the ball in the left section of the rectangle, with movement lines behind it. Draw the background, with the hole to the left of the rectangle. Colour the design in.

3 Indent the three vertical lines of the pop-up, beside the ball and across the movement lines.

4 Cut the horizontal lines, following the shape of the top and bottom of the ball and of the movement lines. Crease all the vertical fold lines and push the pop-up into the card.

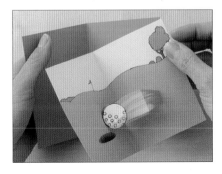

5 Glue to a green backing sheet to complete the card.

Adding an off-centre layer

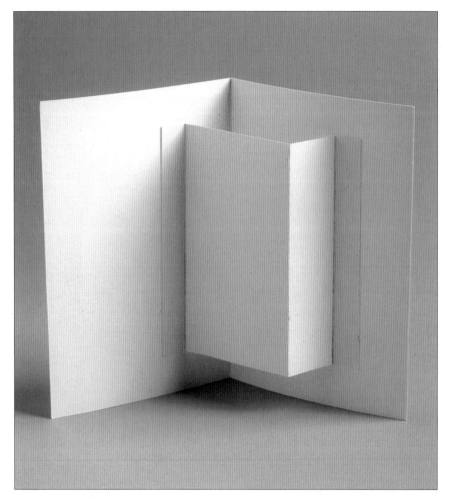

In this technique we move from making a one-piece layer to adding on a layer. You will find this technique, along with adding on V/A folds, extremely useful in creating your own pop-ups.

MATERIALS AND EQUIPMENT
A6 and A7 paper
bone folder
metal ruler
pencil
cutting mat
embossing tool
craft knife
masking tape
glue

1 Fold a sheet of A6 paper widthways and unfold.

> **TIP**
> When making tabs, 1cm/⅜in is usually a good size, but this depends on the size of the pop-up.

2 Mark three vertical fold lines on an A7 sheet with the long edge toward you: two outer lines for the tabs, 1cm/⅜in in from each edge, and a third line for the front corner, which will govern the depth of the pop-up. In this case the pop-up will be 2cm/¾in from the right tab.

3 Indent and crease the fold lines, and attach the left tab 2cm/¾in to the left of the spine.

4 Attach tape to the remaining tab, close the fold and check the position before fixing the tab with glue.

Mouse in cheese

The layer fold is an important mechanism in pop-ups. Here is an example of an off-centre layer with cut-outs to add another dimension.

MATERIALS AND EQUIPMENT
20 x 10cm/8 x 4in thin card (stock)
bone folder
metal ruler
pencil
yellow paper
cutting mat
craft knife
circle template
embossing tool
glue
felt-tipped pens

1 Fold the card in half widthways and unfold. Mark vertical lines 3cm/1³⁄₁₆in to the left of the spine and 6cm/2¼in to the right of it.

2 Cut two rectangles of yellow paper, one 11 x 7cm/4⅜ x 2¾in, and the other 9 x 7cm/3½ x 2¾in. Mark a vertical fold line 1cm/⅜in from each end of the larger piece for tabs, and another 3cm/1³⁄₁₆in from the right tab. Mark a vertical fold line 3cm/1³⁄₁₆in from the left edge on the smaller piece.

TIP
Tabs can be slotted into the page and glued to the back for neatness.

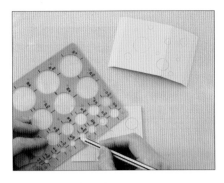

3 Draw circles of various sizes over the cheese, making sure one or two fall over the corner fold line of the pop-up section. Indent the fold lines on each piece.

4 Cut out the circles and part-cut the ones to be reverse-folded. The tabs can be shortened a little to make the pop-up look neater.

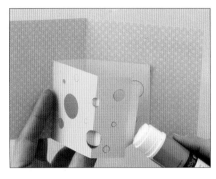

5 Glue the inside of the cheese to the card, followed by the pop-up section with the tabs. Reverse-fold the circles cut on the fold line by pushing them through.

6 Draw and cut out the mouse, and glue in position on the inside of the cheese so that it can be seen through a hole.

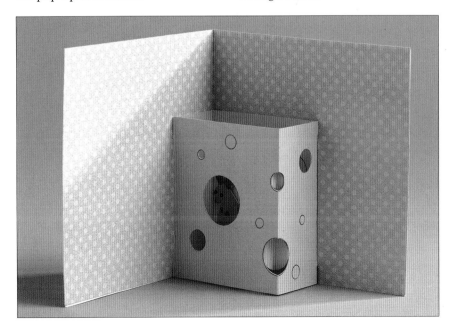

Rectangular slit fold

This is an interesting variation on the layer fold, and if an asymmetric shape is used rather than a rectangle it creates fascinating sculptural effects.

MATERIALS AND EQUIPMENT
A6 paper
metal ruler
pencil
cutting mat
embossing tool
craft knife

1 Turn the long edge of the paper towards you and mark out the central spine, but don't fold it.

2 Draw an off-centre rectangle with the left side 2cm/¾in from the spine. Draw horizontal lines across the rectangle: the distance between them can be as wide or as narrow as you like.

3 Indent the vertical lines of the rectangle and the spine above and below it. Indent a vertical line 2cm/¾in from the right side of the rectangle also.

4 Cut the outer horizontal lines of the rectangle and fold the indented lines before cutting the inner horizontal lines, to make for easier folding. Carefully fold the pop-up to test.

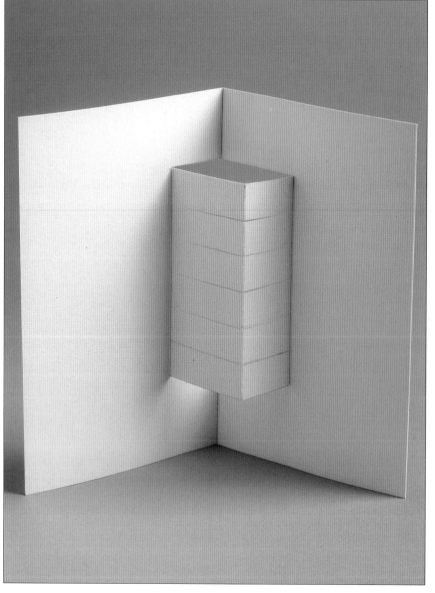

Mayan pyramid

This pyramid is simple to make but looks spectacular in gold paper. If you are using paper-backed gold foil, cut the horizontal lines from the front of the foil to get a neat, smooth result.

MATERIALS AND EQUIPMENT
A5 blue paper
bone folder
pair of compasses
cutting mat
craft knife
metal ruler
pencil
paper-backed gold foil
embossing tool
glue

1 Fold the blue paper in half to make a spine, unfold it and draw a semicircle with a diameter of 21cm/8⅜in. Cut it out. Draw and cut out a second semicircle of the same size and set aside to use as a backing sheet.

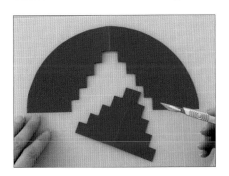

2 Mark and cut out a stepped pyramid shape 10cm/4in wide at the base. Each step is 1.5cm/⅝in high and 1cm/⅜in wide.

3 Using the cut-out as a guide, draw an identical pyramid on the paper backing of a gold sheet (with the spine fold marked). Draw in each horizontal line – these will be cut lines.

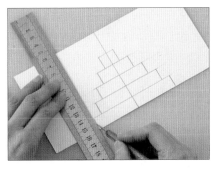

4 Still working on the back of the gold sheet, indent the vertical fold lines at each end of each step.

5 Turn the sheet over and cut the horizontal lines on the front using the indented vertical lines as a guide.

6 Fold all indented lines, cut away the excess paper around the edge and glue the coloured background sheet in front. Add the backing sheet behind the pyramid, otherwise the card will not stand up.

Circular slit fold

This fold uses the same technique as in the last project, but it is interesting to see a rounded shape develop instead of an angular one.

MATERIALS AND EQUIPMENT
A6 paper
bone folder
pair of compasses
metal ruler
pencil
cutting mat
embossing tool
craft knife

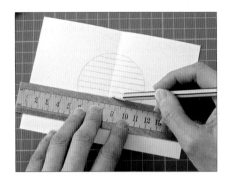

1 Fold the paper in half widthways and unfold it. Draw a circle on the spine with compasses, then mark out horizontal lines from top to bottom. You will get a better effect if the lines are fairly close together.

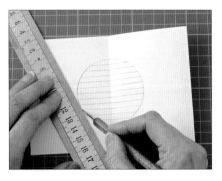

2 Indent the circumference with a series of adjoining straight lines. This will ensure that the paper folds correctly.

3 Cut along all the horizontal lines. At the top and bottom, cut along the curve of the circle, ensuring that you leave a section uncut at each end.

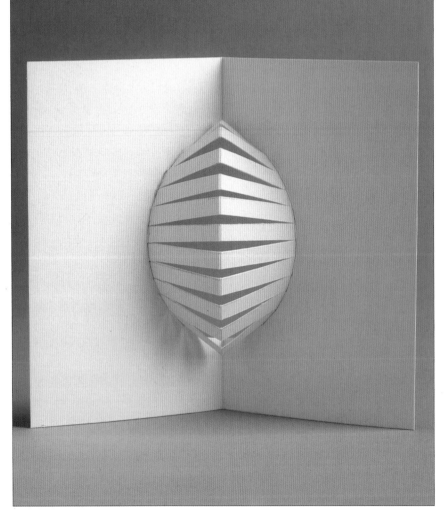

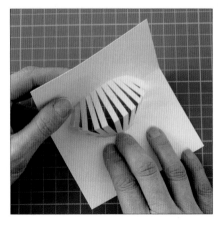

4 Gently push in at each end of the horizontal cuts to finish.

Valentine's heart

Slit folds can take any number of shapes; this example is for Valentine's Day. This card is A6 size, but it can also be made on a larger scale.

MATERIALS AND EQUIPMENT
A6 patterned and red paper
bone folder
metal ruler
pencil
pair of compasses
cutting mat
craft knife
glitter paper
embossing tool
red paint and fine brush or felt-
    tipped pen (optional)
glue

1 For the background, fold the A6 paper widthways and open flat. On the back, draw a central 4cm/1½in square, and within this draw a heart shape. The fold will be smooth if the lines that form the point of the heart are straight.

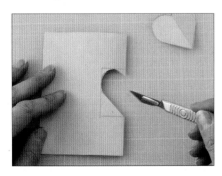

2 Re-fold the paper and cut out the heart, then open out again.

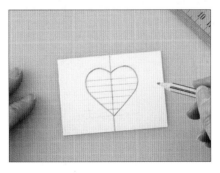

3 Mark the spine on the back of the glitter paper and draw the heart centred on it, using the background as a template. Mark horizontal lines every 5mm/¼in up the heart, but make sure the upper curves of the heart remain together in one section.

TIP
Try not to fold and re-fold special-effect papers too much, as some foils scrape off at the slightest touch.

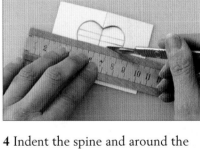

4 Indent the spine and around the outline of the heart, then cut the horizontal lines. If the white backing paper shows between the slits from the front, touch this up carefully with red paint or felt-tipped pen.

5 Fold the heart and place behind the background. Check the fit then glue together, but don't glue too close to the spine to allow a little movement on opening and closing. Add a red backing sheet, which will form the cover of the card.

Advanced folds and cards

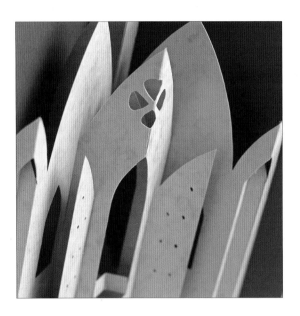

This chapter builds upon the skills learned in the previous section and introduces some more challenging, practical techniques that, when mastered, will yield impressive results.
It includes useful techniques that can be applied to your own designs, such as creating floating and interlocking layers or making multiple V/A folds, and gives tips on using tabs and slots.
The exciting designs include a beautiful and intricate pop-up Russian doll, an elegant and festive pop-up abbey, and a deliciously fun pop-up cupcake that will burst from its box to the surprise and delight of any recipient.

Multiple layer fold

This technique is also known as the step fold, and with a little experimentation, quite intricate step effects can be created.

MATERIALS AND EQUIPMENT
A5 paper
metal ruler
pencil
eraser
cutting mat
embossing tool
craft knife

1 With the long edge of the paper toward you, draw the central spine on the back – do not fold it. Mark the line with a small cross at the top and bottom to save confusion later.

2 Three overlapping rectangles are needed, all 8cm/3⅛in high and 7cm/2¾in, 6cm/2⅜in and 5cm/2in wide. Draw the first one 2cm/¾in from the top of the page, with the right vertical 1.5cm/⁹⁄₁₆in to the right of the spine. Now add an equal amount of 1.5cm/⁹⁄₁₆in to the width on the left side.

3 Erase the spine line within the rectangle. This helps to prevent confusion and potential mistakes in folding later on.

4 Draw the second rectangle 1cm/⅜in lower and with the right vertical 1.5cm/⁹⁄₁₆in further to the right. Add the corresponding width to the left side as before. Erase any pencil lines within this rectangle that relate to the previous one or the spine.

TIP
If you are having problems with the shape not folding, it may be because you have either missed out a cut line, or one has not been cut long enough.

5 Repeat the process described in step 4 for the remaining rectangle.

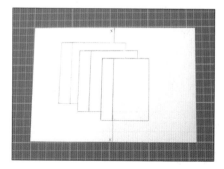

6 Your paper should now be fully marked up for cutting and folding. Check your lines against the image above to ensure it is properly marked.

7 The cut lines are the three horizontal lines across the top of the rectangles (including the top of the border to the left of each one), and the base line, which includes two steps. The remaining vertical lines are fold lines. Indent all the fold lines and cut the horizontals and the base.

8 Fold each indent line, alternating mountain and valley folds as the shape requires; crease the spine at the top and bottom and push the steps through to the front. Your finished multiple layer fold should look like the image of the completed model below.

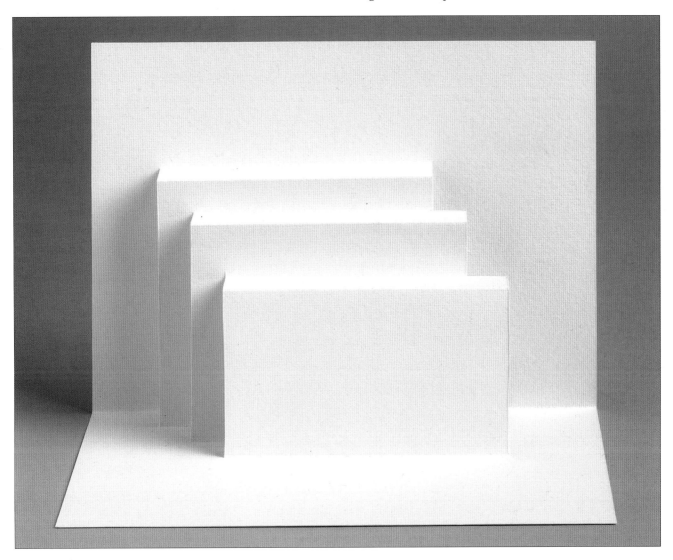

Russian dolls

If you take the theory of the multiple layer fold and turn it inside out, this is the kind of result you might get – instead of the layers coming forward, they recede. The Russian dolls design can be adapted for other characters, such as a family, footballers, farmyard animals or jungle creatures.

MATERIALS AND EQUIPMENT
A4 paper and coloured card (stock)
metal ruler
pencil
cutting mat
embossing tool
tracing paper
felt-tipped pens
craft knife
glue
bone folder

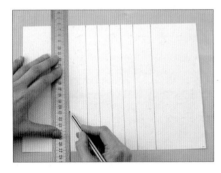

1 With the paper in landscape mode, draw the spine and mark out vertical fold lines for the three layers, at the following distances from the spine on each side: 2cm/¾in, 4cm/1½in and 7cm/2¾in.

TIP
This design can be used to create an impressive and highly decorative set of greetings cards. Trace the design of the first card at the end of step 5, and then transfer it across to all of the other cards in the set.

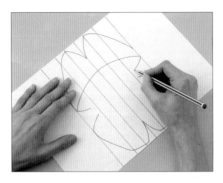

2 Draw the largest doll first, as an oval shape at the top and bottom with a large gap in the middle; it can be up to 20cm/8in high and as wide as your outside guidelines. The curved shape near the spine at the top and bottom will give a rounded effect to the layer.

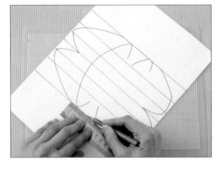

3 Indent the outer fold line from the top to the bottom of the part where the design touches this line. Indent the next line in also, but this time only indent the section that falls inside the open doll. Repeat with the other lines.

4 Draw the outlines of the remaining two dolls (there is no need to draw the central curves to shape them) and rub out the vertical lines.

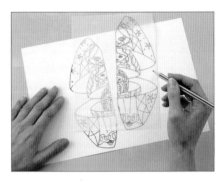

5 Fill in the detail of the design on one side, then transfer it to the other side using tracing paper and colour it in.

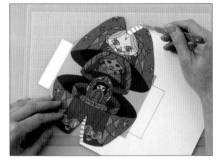

6 Cut around the outside doll, leaving an 8cm/3⅛in section in the middle of each side to make tabs to attach to the background. When you come to the curves at the top and bottom of the spine, draw a few tabs on one side and cut around them so that you can glue them under the other side.

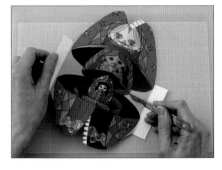

7 Cut the opening edges of the two outer dolls and fold the vertical indent lines where they fall inside the next biggest doll.

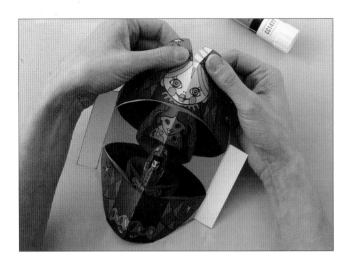

8 Glue the tabs at the top and bottom curve of the outside doll. Re-crease the fold lines in alternate valley and mountain folds.

9 Fold an A4 sheet of coloured card in half widthways, then cut slits to fit the vertical tabs 6cm/2¼in either side of the spine. Insert the tabs and secure them on the back.

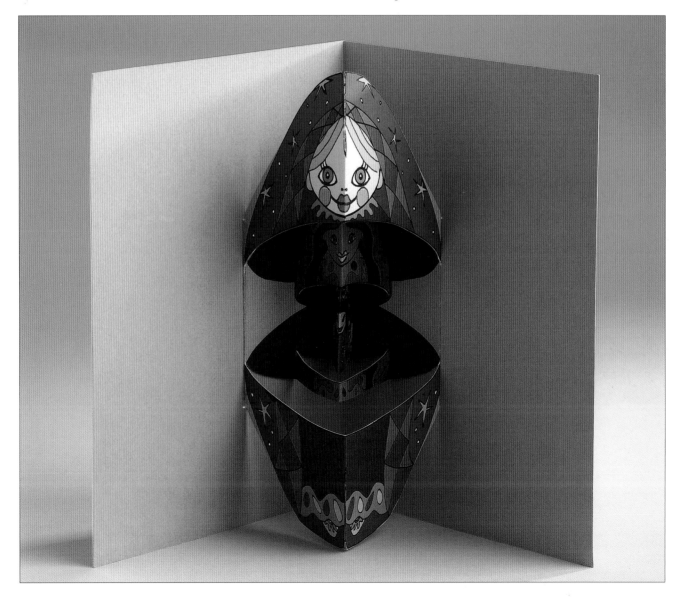

Multiple V/A folds

Multiple V/A folds require the pop-ups to be added on as separate pieces. This gives limitless scope for scenery, figures, objects or even greetings messages.

MATERIALS AND EQUIPMENT
A6 paper
bone folder
protractor
pencil
metal ruler
cutting mat
embossing tool
craft knife
masking tape
glue

1 Fold the paper in half widthways and open out. Mark three A shapes, which can be at any distance apart, along the spine. Experiment with the angles: here they are at 35° from the spine.

3 Still with the paper folded, indent a diagonal line from the spine to the outside edge in each section, so you end up with a triangle in each section. These will be at approximately 45°, but you can vary this angle for differing effects (see Tip) depending on the project that you are making.

TIP
If an angle of more than 45° is used for the add-ons, more care is needed to ensure they do not protrude from the closed fold, although the bigger the angle, the more dramatic the pop-up.

2 Fold another sheet of paper lengthways, then divide it into three equal sections with pencil lines: these will be cut lines.

4 Mark a cut line 1cm/⅜in above and parallel with each of the diagonal indented lines.

  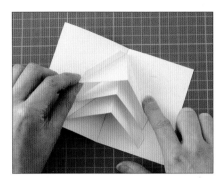

5 Cut firmly along the horizontal and diagonal cut lines using a scalpel and ruler; this will leave you with three identical A folds with protruding tabs.

6 Tape the tabs temporarily to the guidelines and check that they are all folding correctly. The pieces should not rub together if all the angles are the same.

7 Attach the tabs to the paper permanently with glue, being careful to line them up with the guidelines. As these are add-ons you will not need to add a backing sheet.

Congratulations!

This version of multiple V folds has two layers, so there is plenty of space to add a greeting inside the card, but you can add as many layers as you can fit in for a greater impact. This is a design for a generic celebration card, but this technique could easily be adapted to suit any occasion.

MATERIALS AND EQUIPMENT
A4 gold mirror card and thin white card (stock)
bone folder
protractor
metal ruler
embossing tool
A4 tracing paper
pencil
felt-tipped pens
cutting mat
craft knife
glue

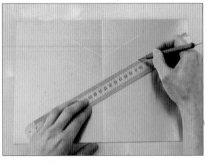

1 Fold the card in half widthways to form the base. With an embossing tool, mark two Vs starting 6.5cm/2½in and 11.5cm/4½in from the top of the spine, at angles of 60°.

TIP
You may want to practise marking up the guides for the base on scrap paper first, as any mistakes made when marking or drawing on mirror card cannot be erased.

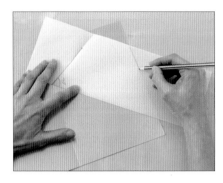

2 To make the bottle layer, fold a sheet of tracing paper in half lengthways, and on each side of the spine, near the bottom draw base lines 8cm/3⅛in long at an angle of 70°. Place the tracing on the card, aligning the base line with one side of the top V, and mark out the section that will fall inside the closed card. The spine length will be about 15cm/6in.

3 Draw the bottle inside the marked area and above the angled lines at the base. Add surrounding objects over the tab area; this will provide support.

4 Transfer the design on to thin card and colour it, making sure the base lines are visible, then cut it out.

5 Repeat for the foremost layer. As it is further down the card, it needs more width and less height – the spine should be 11cm/4½in. Draw the glasses overlapping the spine – there should be a small area of spine between them, at least 3mm/⅛in, which will remain uncut.

6 Transfer the design on to thin card and colour it, making sure the spine and the angled base lines are visible.

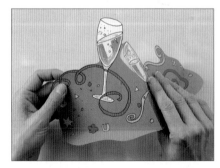

7 Cut out, carefully cutting around the section of the glass that overlaps the opposite side, but keeping the spine intact. Indent and fold the spine and base lines, but don't indent where the edges of the glasses overlap the spine.

8 Check that the first layer fits neatly along the upper base line of the mirror card that forms the base of the pop-up. When you are happy with the fit, glue it firmly in place along the upper base line.

9 Attach the second layer in the same way. Both layers can have more decorative cuts so that they look less solid, but take care not to cut too much away or the pop-up will not be strong enough to stand up.

Interlocking layers

Here is another version of multiple layers, but adding on interlocking pieces to extend the pop. Any number of pieces can be linked in this way, but take care to check how far the pieces jut out when folded.

MATERIALS AND EQUIPMENT
A6 and A5 paper
bone folder
metal ruler
pencil
cutting mat
embossing tool
craft knife

3 Inside the largest rectangle, draw fold lines for 1cm/⅜in tabs running down both sides, and draw cut lines as follows: two 4.5cm/1¾in vertical lines 5cm/2in from the spine – from the top down on one side and from the bottom up on the other; and two 3cm/1³⁄₁₆in vertical lines, 3cm/1³⁄₁₆in from the spine on each side and both from the top down.

1 Fold the A6 paper in half widthways, unfold and mark tabs at 1cm/⅜in from the spine on each side. These need to be 9cm/3½in long and run up from the bottom of the sheet.

2 On A5 paper, with the short edge toward you, draw a spine and three rectangles centred on the spine: the largest 14cm/5½in wide and 9cm/3½in high, the next 8cm/3⅛in wide and 6cm/2¼in high, and the third 6cm/2¼in wide and 3cm/1³⁄₁₆in high.

4 Inside the medium rectangle draw two 3cm/1³⁄₁₆in cut lines from the top down, 3cm/1³⁄₁₆in from the spine, and two 1.5cm/⁹⁄₁₆in lines from the bottom up, 2cm/¾in from the spine.

> **TIP**
> The length of the interlocking cut lines is determined by the size of the smaller pop-up element – each cut line should be exactly half the length of the smaller piece.

5 In the smallest rectangle, draw two cut lines 1.5cm/⁹⁄₁₆in long, and 1cm/⅜in from the spine at the top.

6 Cut out the rectangles, cutting the largest one in half along its centre line.

7 Cut all the drawn cut lines. Indent the tab lines and the spines of the two smaller pieces. Interlock the two tall tabbed rectangles and glue them to the tab markings on the A6 page, with the remaining interlock lines pointing down.

8 Fold the second rectangle at the indented line and, using the outer interlock lines, slot into the tall rectangles. Repeat this step with the remaining rectangle to finish.

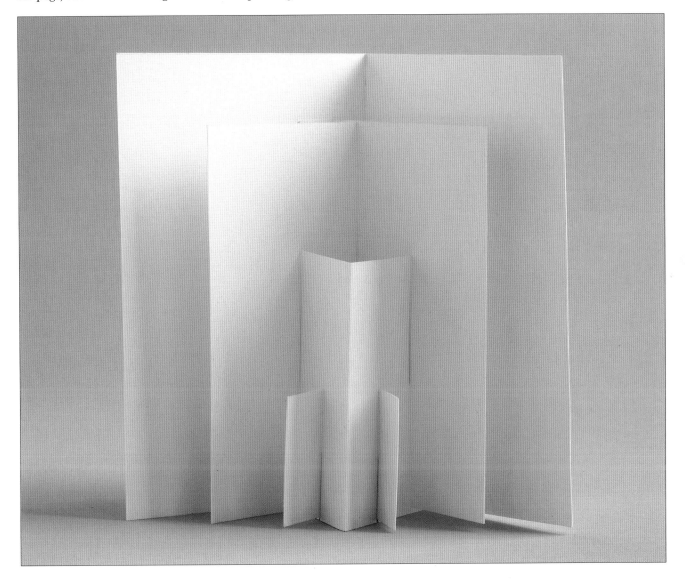

Abbey

This uses exactly the same technique as the interlocking layers on the previous pages, with the same number of pieces, but the additional folds, shapes and cut-outs make it a little more complicated. However, the stunning effect is worth the extra effort.

MATERIALS AND EQUIPMENT
A4 coloured and white paper
bone folder
metal ruler
pencil
cutting mat
craft knife
A4 medium pale grey card (stock)
embossing tool
masking tape
glue

1 Fold the coloured paper in half widthways to make the backing sheet, then unfold and draw vertical lines 2cm/¾in, 6cm/2¼in and 12cm/4¾in from the spine fold on both sides, to mark the tab positions.

TIP
The simple, elegant lines and muted colours of this design create an impressive end result, but if you want a more colourful pop-up you could experiment with tissue paper to create a stained-glass effect in the windows.

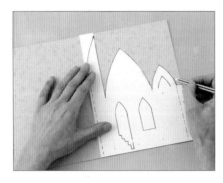

2 Draw a template for one side of the first layer, 16cm/6⅜in wide (including a 1cm/⅜in tab each side) and 21cm/8⅜in high. The tops of the central half-arch and two further arches are at 2cm/¾in, 6cm/2¼in and 12cm/4¾in from the centre line; the wide arch is 18cm/7in tall and the outer arch is 14cm/5½in. All start 10cm/4in from the bottom. Add the window and door. Cut out the template and draw round it on the grey card, turning it over to draw the second side. Cut out the two pieces.

3 Mark the positions for the interlocking cuts. Under the point of the central half-arch mark a 5cm/2in line from the top down on one side and from the bottom up on the other. At the centre of the wide arch, mark a 5cm/2in line from the bottom up on each side. Draw a smaller arch inside each of the small arches; indent the vertical lines and cut around the top curves.

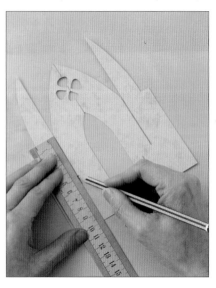

4 The middle section is 14cm/5½in wide (including 1cm/⅜in tabs on each side) and consists of a single 17cm/6⅝in arch with a central doorway and decorative window above. Fold the card in half widthways to create a spine and draw a central doorway 3cm/1³⁄₁₆in wide and 11cm/4⅜in high. Within this, draw one or two steps, and add the decorative window feature. Add 5cm/2in interlock lines on both sides of the archway: from the top down at 4cm/1½in from the spine, and from the bottom up at 2.5cm/1in from the spine. Cut around the template and interlock lines.

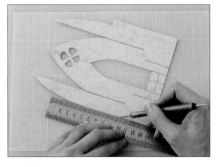

5 Indent the spine and the two outer tabs, which will be attached to the backing sheet.

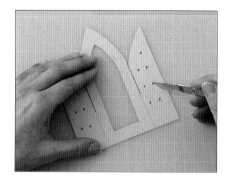

6 The final section is a central arch with an open door on either side of it, 11cm/4⅜in wide x 13cm/5in high, with no tabs. Fold the card in half vertically and draw half the arch, ending at 7cm/2¾in high and 2.5cm/1in from the spine. From that point, draw the arch of the open door up to 11cm/4⅜in high and a downward interlock line 3.5cm/1⅜in long.

9 Slot the central arched doorway into the first layer and attach the tabs to the coloured backing sheet. Attach the outer tabs on the back layer to the sheet.

10 Finally, slot the remaining door section into the doorway, and make any final adjustments that are necessary before gluing the tabs permanently.

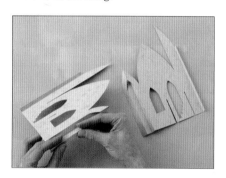

7 Cut the slots and door opening. Then, create a door decoration by cutting small ornamental holes in the two open doors. Fold the indented lines on all pieces and reverse-fold the end arches.

8 Slot the back pieces together and attach the inner tabs to the backing sheet at the marked positions.

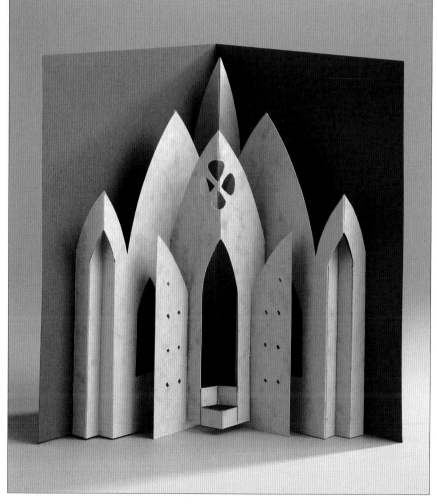

Floating layers

This useful and adaptable technique is similar to the layering methods that we have already covered, with the additional effect that the elements appear to be floating in a mysterious way. This illusion looks stunning, and people may wonder how it is achieved - in fact it is simply done by placing the interlocking layers on "legs".

MATERIALS AND EQUIPMENT
A6 and A7 paper
bone folder
metal ruler
pencil
cutting mat
craft knife
glue
embossing tool

1 Fold the A6 sheet in half widthways to create a spine.

2 Repeat with an A7 sheet, then cut a slot 3cm/1³⁄₁₆in long, 3cm/1³⁄₁₆in to the left of the spine and parallel with it, from the bottom up. This is layer 1.

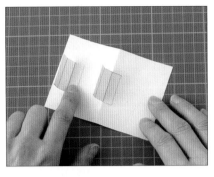

3 Make a tab sheet or create individual tabs – in this case a suitable size would be 3cm/1³⁄₁₆in squares with parallel folds at 1cm/³⁄₈in in from either side. Turn layer 1 over and glue one tab on the spine and one on the uncut side, parallel to the spine.

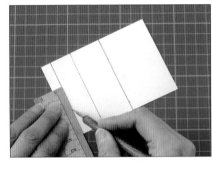

4 With the long edge toward you, take another A7 sheet of paper and carefully score indent lines at 1cm/³⁄₈in, 3cm/1³⁄₁₆in and 6cm/2¼in from the left side of the page. This will form layer 2.

5 Still working on layer 2, cut a 3cm/1³⁄₁₆in vertical slot from the top down, 2cm/¾in from the left.

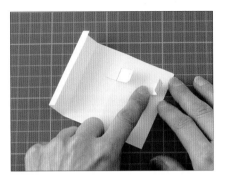

6 Fold the indent lines and add two tabs on the back as before, this time ensuring that they are on the bottom half of the sheet.

7 Slot the two layers together.

TIP
A tab sheet is a very useful, time-saving device. Mark up and pre-fold a sheet of tabs that can simply be cut out when needed – it is a good idea to make up several sheets with differently sized tabs, so that you always have the size you need to hand.

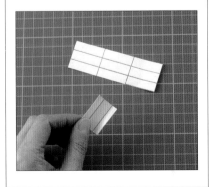

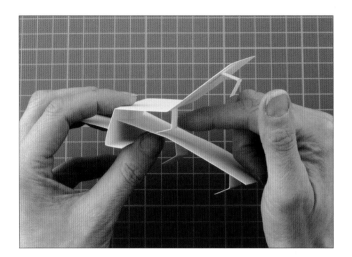

8 Attach the spine tab on layer 2 to layer 1 first, then the other tab parallel to the spine, so the two layers stay together.

9 You will see that the folds on layer 2 have created a third leg and tab to attach to the base sheet. Attach this and all the other tabs.

Floating hearts

This project uses the floating layer technique with additional extensions to add extra interest. Once you get the hang of this technique, each layer can be cut into so that glimpses of the layers below can be seen, and the layers needn't be rectangular.

MATERIALS AND EQUIPMENT
A5 and A6 black paper
metal ruler
pencil
cutting mat
craft knife
glue
red glossy or glitter paper
ready-made stickers

1 Pre-cut a strip of tabs. You will need 12 "legs" to hold each layer invisibly, each 3cm/1³⁄₁₆in long (to allow 1cm/³⁄₈in fixings on each side); the width needs to be less for the smaller layers.

2 Fold a sheet of A5 paper in half widthways for the base. The first layer is A6: fold a central spine, cut out a small heart from the centre and make decorative cuts around the edge.

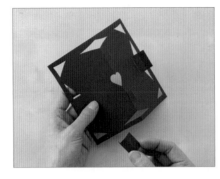

3 Attach four legs to the piece, two to the spine above and below the heart cutout, and one to either side.

4 The second layer is A7. Repeat steps 2 and 3, but this time make the cut-out heart larger than before so you will be able to see the one in the layer below.

5 The third layer is smaller again, while the cut-out heart is larger still. Add supporting legs as before.

TIP
The sizes and shapes of all the layers can be variable.

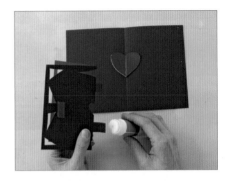

6 Cut a heart from the red paper and glue it in the centre of the backing sheet. Attach the largest layer, gluing the legs at the spine first. Glue each outer leg, point it towards the spine and close the page on it to ensure it is facing the correct way when glued.

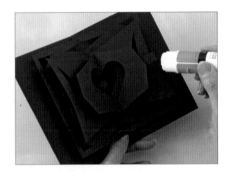

7 Add the next two layers in the same way, attaching the legs with glue as before.

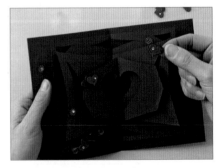

8 Decorate the layers of card with ready-made stickers or small red paper hearts you have cut out yourself, allowing them to overhang the edges so that they appear to be floating.

Tab-held shapes – parallel

The next few techniques create a number of tab-held shapes, from the most basic outlines to circular, enclosed and curved shapes. The first example is a square box with its sides parallel to the edges of the base sheet.

MATERIALS AND EQUIPMENT
A6 paper
bone folder
metal ruler
pencil
cutting mat
embossing tool
craft knife
glue
masking tape

1 Fold a sheet of paper in half widthways, and unfold. In the centre, mark two tab positions 3cm/1³⁄₁₆in long, parallel to the spine and 1.5cm/⁹⁄₁₆in on either side.

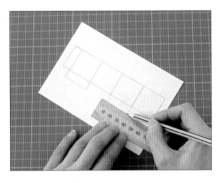

2 To make the pop-up, on another A6 sheet, draw four adjoining 3cm/1³⁄₁₆in squares, with an extra 1cm/³⁄₈in tab at one end. Add 1cm/³⁄₈in tabs to the lower edge of two alternate squares.

3 Use an embossing tool to indent fold lines between all the squares and tabs. In addition, the two squares without attached tabs will fold in half, so indent a vertical fold line down the centre of each.

4 Use a craft knife to cut out the shape, complete with tabs.

5 Fold all the indented lines and assemble the shape by gluing the end tab.

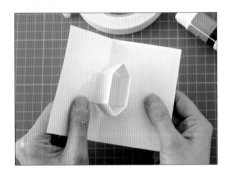

6 Tape the remaining tabs to the marked positions and test that the mechanism is opening correctly before gluing them permanently.

TIP
The central folds in the unattached squares will fold just as easily into the box or outwards, as you prefer.

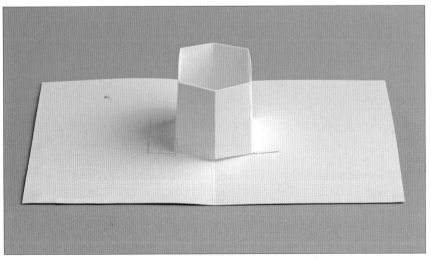

Tab-held shapes – diagonal

This technique is similar to the previous one, but because of the position of the tabs the box needs no extra folds in its sides to fold flat.

MATERIALS AND EQUIPMENT
A6 paper
bone folder
metal ruler
pencil
cutting mat
embossing tool
craft knife
glue
masking tape

1 Fold a sheet of paper in half widthways to make the spine and unfold. Mark two tab positions 3cm/1³⁄₁₆in long, at 45° angles to the spine.

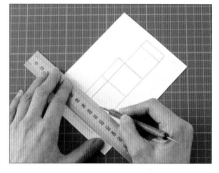

2 To make the pop-up, on another A6 sheet draw four adjoining 3cm/1³⁄₁₆in squares, with an extra 1cm/³⁄₈in tab at one end. Add 1cm/³⁄₈in tabs to the lower edge of two adjacent squares. Indent fold lines between all the squares and tabs.

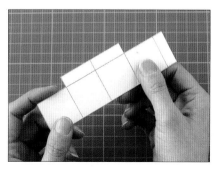

3 Use a craft knife to cut out the shape and cut between the tabs.

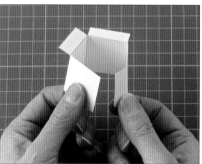

4 Fold all the indented lines and assemble the shape by gluing the end tab.

5 Tape the remaining tabs in the marked positions, and fold the card gently to test that the mechanism is working correctly. Remove the tape and attach the tabs permanently with glue.

Cupcake

A delicious cupcake bursting from a box couldn't be easier to make using coloured and patterned papers – both thick paper and thin card will work well. This idea is just right for a set of party invitations.

MATERIALS AND EQUIPMENT
A5 coloured, patterned and white
   paper or thin card (stock)
bone folder
metal ruler
pencil
cutting mat
craft knife
tracing paper
embossing tool
glue
felt-tipped pens
scraps of coloured paper

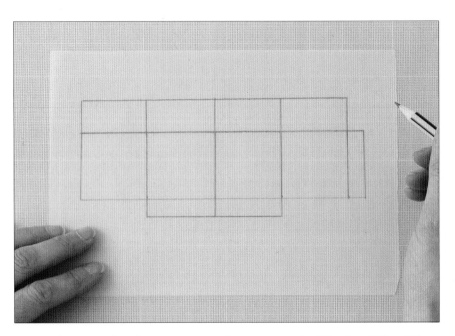

2 To make a template for the pop-up, draw a rectangle 17 x 6cm/6⅝ x 2¼in. Mark off 1cm/⅜in at one end for a tab and divide the rest into four. Mark off 2cm/¾in across the top for the lid sections, and add 1cm/⅜in tabs to the lower edge of two adjacent squares.

1 Fold an A5 coloured sheet in half widthways to make the spine and unfold. Cut two 45° lines just under 4cm/1½in long, beginning a little way from the spine.

3 Transfer the design to patterned paper or card and cut out, cutting between each lid section. Indent fold lines between all the squares and tabs.

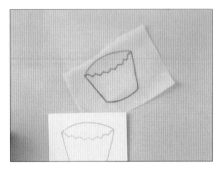

5 Inside a rectangle 4cm/1½in wide and 6cm/2¼in high, draw the cupcake with a 1cm/⅜in tab on each side.

6 Transfer the design to white paper and decorate. Indent the fold lines.

TIPS
• Look out for double-sided card, with a different pattern on each side, to make the box.
• For a neater finish you can add a backing sheet to the finished card – this will prevent the tabs being seen sticking through the back of the card.

4 Assemble by gluing the end tab.

7 Fold back the tabs and glue them to two opposite sides of the box.

8 To finish, slide the bottom tabs on the box into the slots on the base, and secure on the back with glue.

Tab-held shapes – circular

When making a round pop-up shape, the tabs should be placed parallel to the spine to ensure they pull the shape into a full circle; a 45° angle fixing will not work unless you have an enclosed shape, which will be shown later.

MATERIALS AND EQUIPMENT
A6 paper
bone folder
metal ruler
pencil
cutting mat
embossing tool
craft knife
glue
masking tape

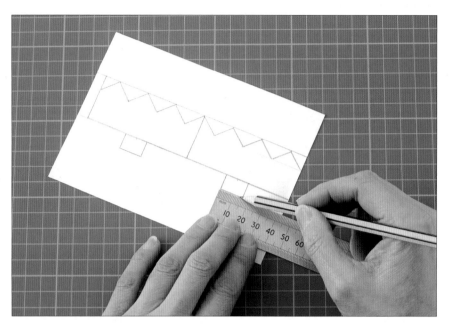

3 Vary the top edge to add interest if you wish, then add two 2cm/¾in tabs along the bottom edge, in the centre of each section.

1 Fold an A6 sheet in half widthways to make the spine and unfold. In the centre, mark two tab positions 2cm/¾in long, parallel to the spine and 2cm/¾in to either side.

4 Indent the fold lines and cut out the shape, complete with tabs.

2 To make the pop-up, on another A6 sheet draw a rectangle 13 x 3cm/5 x 1³⁄₁₆in, and within this mark the vertical fold lines at 6cm/2⁵⁄₁₆in and 12cm/4⅝in.

TIP
Experiment with varying the circumference and the height of the pop-up, always bearing in mind its folded size when closed. This would suit a Rapunzel's tower; if the top of the tower is to be narrower this can be achieved by making the piece in two halves and gluing together at the folded edges.

5 Fold all the indented lines and assemble the shape by gluing the end tab.

6 Tape the remaining tabs to the marked positions and test that the mechanism works before gluing permanently.

Flower

This project shows what can be achieved with a simple technique by varying the angles of the circular pop-up and adding some extra layers.

MATERIALS AND EQUIPMENT
A5 handmade paper
bone folder
metal ruler
pencil
cutting mat
craft knife
tracing paper
pair of compasses
yellow paper
embossing tool
glue

1 Fold a sheet of A5 handmade paper in half widthways and unfold. Mark tab positions in the centre, parallel with the spine, at 1cm/⅜in and 7mm/¼in to either side, and cut slits at the markings.

2 On tracing paper, draw a 12cm/4¾in diameter circle, with an inner circle of 3cm/1³⁄₁₆in diameter, and divide into eight equal sections.

3 Draw petals in six of the sections, making sure they meet well outside the inner circle, which will be cut away. Add tabs in the inner circle on the second and fifth petal, and a joining tab along the edge of a petal on one end.

4 Transfer the flower shape to yellow paper, and indent a valley fold between each petal and along the tabs.

5 Cut out the shape, crease the folds and join the petals together by gluing the tab.

6 On tracing paper, draw another 12cm/4¾in diameter circle, with an inner circle of 3cm/1³⁄₁₆in. Divide half the circle into six sections for the inner petals, which will have a wavy edge. The other half is for the stamens – leave it untouched for now.

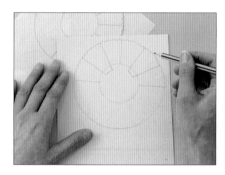

7 Transfer the shape to yellow paper, adding tabs in the centre circle as before on the second and fifth petals. Indent the fold lines on the inner petals and tabs.

8 Cut out the inner petals, cutting away the inner circle except the tabs. On the other semicircle, cut slits all the way around for the stamens.

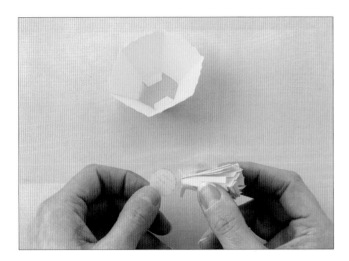

9 Assemble the inner petals by gluing the joining tab as before. Next, roll up the inner stamens and glue together. Cut small tabs and attach to a circle of paper, which should be small enough to fit in between the tab markings on the page and also have a spine fold.

10 Finally, glue the tabs to the page at the points marked, beginning with the outer petals and working inwards; end by gluing the circle attached to the stamens into the centre.

Enclosed curved shapes

It is possible to add a curve to a tab-held shape, creating a wonderfully three-dimensional structure.

MATERIALS AND EQUIPMENT
A5 paper
bone folder
metal ruler
pencil
pair of compasses
cutting mat
embossing tool
craft knife
glue
masking tape

3 Enlarge the radius of the compasses by 1cm/⅜ and draw another curve from the same point on one side of the circumference to add a tab section along the inside edge of one of the eye shapes.

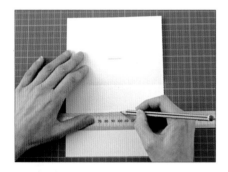

1 Fold an A5 sheet in half widthways to make the spine, and unfold. In the centre, mark two tab positions 2cm/¾in long, parallel to the spine and 4cm/1½in to either side.

4 Divide the extra section into smaller tabs, and add a 2 x 1cm/¾ x ⅜in tab to the centre of the outer edge of each shape.

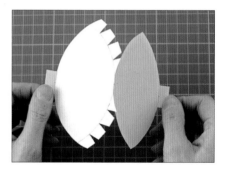

6 Cut around the shape and fold the crease lines, then open the shape out flat.

2 On another sheet, draw a circle with a radius of 5cm/2in. Place the compass point on the circumference and draw part of another circle within the first, then repeat on the opposite side to give two identical "eye" shapes touching in the middle.

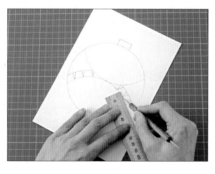

5 Indent all the tab fold lines using a metal ruler and an embossing tool.

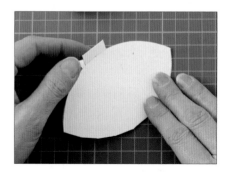

7 Glue the joining tabs, fold the shape and tuck in all the tabs, ensuring a smooth join.

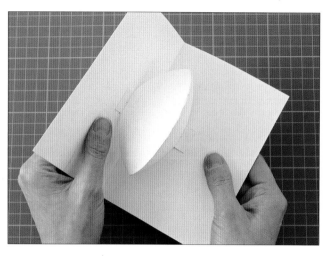

8 Tape one of the outer tabs to the position marked on the base sheet, add tape to the remaining tab and close the fold.

9 Check that the pop-up movement is working correctly, then glue the tabs to the background sheet to attach them permanently.

Boat at sea

This project combines some of the tab-held shapes you have already learned, using enclosed and curved shapes to make a little boat ploughing through the waves. For a watery effect you can cut out some ripples from green paper and glue them to the base around the boat.

MATERIALS AND EQUIPMENT
A5 paper in blue-green, white
  and red
bone folder
metal ruler
pencil
protractor
cutting mat
craft knife
embossing tool
glue

1 Fold a sheet of blue-green paper in half widthways and unfold. Mark 4cm/1½in tab positions for the boat, parallel with the spine, at 1cm/⅜in and 2cm/¾in to either side. For the big wave, draw two 6cm/2¼in lines at 30° to the spine, starting no less than 3cm/1³⁄₁₆in from the bottom.

TIP
For a neater finish, add a backing sheet to the reverse of this pop-up. This will conceal the tabs that have been slotted through the page and glued to the other side.

2 The cabin section is an enclosed rectangle, which can be drawn as one long shape: the height is 4cm/1½in, the long sides are 4cm/1½in wide, the short sides 2cm/¾in wide and the roof sections are attached to the long sides. Add a tab down one side and at the base of each long side; draw a funnel in the centre of the roof, with tabs on each side, and add portholes to the sides of the cabin.

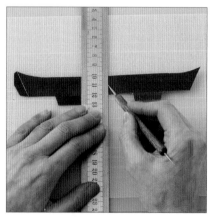

3 Draw and cut out the hull in one piece from red paper, indenting a vertical fold at the stern. Each side is 8cm/3⅛in long at the base (9.5cm/3¾in at the top) and 3cm/1³⁄₁₆in high, rising to 4.5cm/1¾in at the bow, where there is a joining tab. Add a 3cm/1³⁄₁₆in base tab to each side.

4 Draw the wave on white paper as two mirror image pieces, 10cm/4in long and 4cm/1½in high at the front, with a curve and a wavy line tapering down to the end. Add page tabs with wavy edges and small joining tabs on one side of the front curve. Indent the tabs and around the curve, and cut out the pieces.

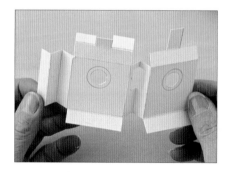

5 Indent the fold lines between the cabin walls, halfway folds on the short sides, and the tabs. Cut out the cabin, including the portholes, and fold the indent lines.

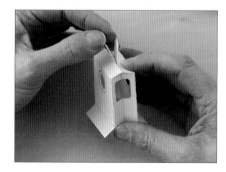

6 Assemble the cabin by gluing the tabs at the side and on the roof.

7 Indent all fold lines for the hull and assemble by gluing the end tab.

8 Attach the assembled cabin section to the inner tab positions on the base sheet.

9 Slip the hull section over the cabin and attach the tabs to the outer tab markings, checking to see that it folds correctly. For a neater finish, cut slits at the marked positions to take the tabs.

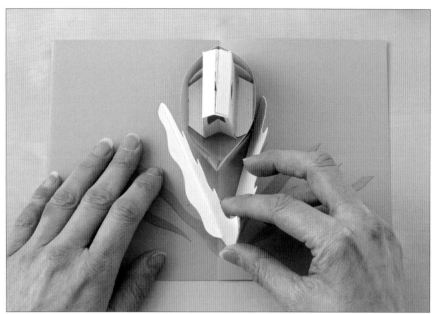

10 Finally, glue the wave pieces together and attach the base tabs to the marked positions. There are no tabs at the end of the wave but you will find that if you add glue to the outside of the wave and attach it to the page, this will pull the shape back and add to the movement.

Spirals

This easy project demonstrates different ways you can use spirals in your pop-ups. Try using a brightly coloured or even black backing sheet, which will show the spirals up more effectively.

MATERIALS AND EQUIPMENT
A4 and A6 paper
bone folder
glue
pair of compasses
pencil
cutting mat
craft knife
masking tape

3 Glue the small layer to the top of the base sheet, with the tabs about 2cm/¾in either side of the spine, so that when the page is open the piece stands upright.

1 Fold an A4 sheet in half widthways to create a spine.

2 Fold an A6 sheet in half widthways, then add another fold 1cm/⅜in in from each end to make tabs.

4 Single-line spirals, as the name suggests, are cut out along a single line, producing tight shapes with many curls. Draw a 6cm/2¼in diameter circle using compasses, then draw a single line spiralling into the centre. Repeat to make three spirals.

TIP
Try experimenting with irregularly shaped spirals, such as ovals and squares. You can also make smaller shapes to thread on to the spirals, which will create more movement.

5 For double-line spirals, draw two parallel lines, coming together at the end and in the centre. The area between the two lines is cut away, giving a more open shape. Cut out all the spirals.

6 Try different ways of attaching the spirals. Glue one end of a spiral to the layer, add tape to the other end and close the page. Now, see the difference when the spiral is attached to both sides of the base page so it opens fully.

7 The spirals can be lengthened by joining them end to end (at the centres or the ends) and then attaching to the page: as they are longer they need to be glued nearer the edges of the page.

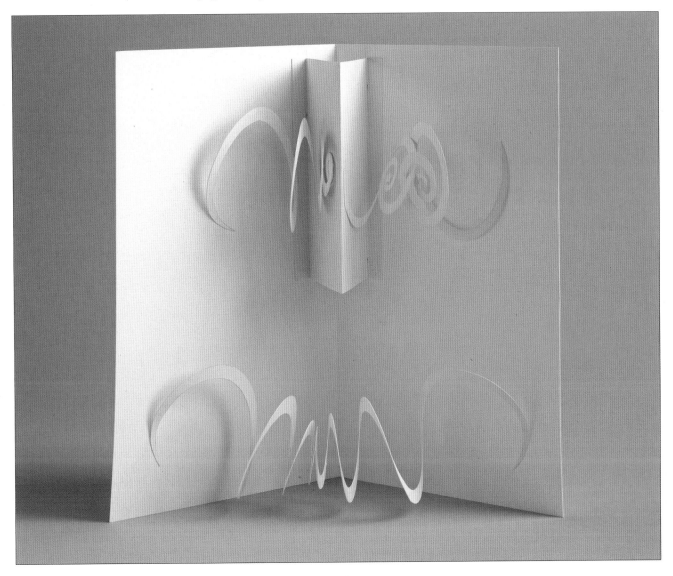

Octopus

Using spirals gives wonderful freeform effects, put to good use in this octopus pop-up. As it is quite hard to judge where the spirals will fall and end up, it is a good idea to make this as a rough first, which will give you a template to use for the final colour version.

MATERIALS AND EQUIPMENT
A4 coloured and double-sided
   patterned paper
bone folder
metal ruler
pencil
A4 tracing paper
felt-tipped pens or paper scraps to
   decorate
cutting mat
embossing tool
craft knife
glue
masking tape

2 Add some tentacles, which can be drawn on the page or cut out of patterned paper and glued on below the tab markings. In this case, five tentacles will be spirals, so draw three on the background page.

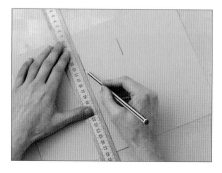

1 Fold a coloured A4 sheet in half widthways. Draw two tab positions 4cm/1½in long, parallel to the spine near the top, 3.5cm/1⅜in to either side.

> **TIP**
> Cut experimental spirals from a sheet of paper identical in size to your folded card; this will ensure that they will not jut out when the card is folded.

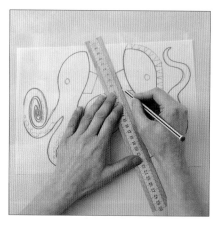

3 Fold a sheet of A4 tracing paper in half widthways. Draw half the octopus on one side, with two spiral tentacles and a vertical tab of 4cm/1½in at the edge of the body.

4 Transfer the drawing to the other half of the paper, this time adding joining tabs along the front of the body. The tentacles can be in different positions on this half. Draw a separate spiral, which will be attached to one of the tentacles later.

5 Transfer the drawings on to patterned paper and decorate as you like.

6 Indent the tab lines and cut out all the pieces. Cut slots at the marked positions in the background page.

7 Glue the tabs at the front of the body and join the pieces together.

8 Slide the body tabs into the slots on the page and temporarily secure them with low-tack tape at the back.

9 Glue the ends of the spiral tentacles to the background, almost closing the page to position them. Add the separate spiral tentacle, attaching it halfway along the top left tentacle and also to the page.

Rotating disc technique

By means of a layer with an A fold and a rotating disc, a fantastic three-dimensional circular movement can be achieved.

MATERIALS AND EQUIPMENT
A5 paper
bone folder
metal ruler
pencil
cutting mat
embossing tool
craft knife
glue
pair of compasses

3 From the middle of the 8.5cm/3⅜in line, mark an A fold 3cm/1³⁄₁₆in wide and 2.5cm/1in high. Extend the left side of the A shape downwards 1–2cm/⅜–¾in – the disc will be attached to this area.

1 Fold the paper in half widthways and mark two vertical tab positions, 1.5cm/⁹⁄₁₆in to the left and 6cm/2¼in to the right of the spine.

2 On another sheet, draw a rectangle 13cm/5in wide and 8cm/3⅛in high. Inside this, mark vertical fold lines at 1cm/⅜in, 7cm/2¾in, 8.5cm/3⅜in and 10cm/4in from the left.

4 Indent all the vertical fold lines and the A fold lines with an embossing tool. Cut out the rectangle with a craft knife.

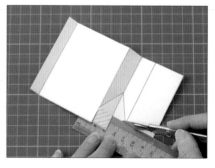

5 Cut the bottom of the A fold, including the longer leg on the left.

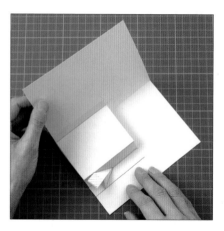

6 Attach the side tabs of the layer to the tab positions on the page, folding the layer in the page and folding the A fold so that it sticks outwards.

TIP
The size of the layer and the disc can vary, as can the positioning of the disc. Use masking tape to fix the disc in different positions to see how it alters the movement.

7 Using compasses, draw a disc 7cm/2¾in in diameter and cut it out with a craft knife or scissors – use whichever you find gives the neatest result.

8 Glue the disc to the extending part of the A fold only, positioning the centre of the disc nearest the top point of the A fold, which is the centre of the rotation.

Rocking horse

Applying the rotating disc technique to this project gives the perfect rocking movement for the horse, but it could just as easily be used for turning wheels, the back legs of animals or even just animating a text greeting.

MATERIALS AND EQUIPMENT
A5 patterned paper
bone folder
metal ruler
pencil
cutting mat
craft knife
embossing tool
glue
tracing paper
paints or scraps of white and
    coloured paper
masking tape

1 Fold a sheet of patterned paper in half widthways and mark two tab positions, 1.5cm/⁹⁄₁₆in to the left and 6cm/2¼in to the right of the spine.

TIP
The depth of the layer and that of the A fold will vary the rotation; a wider layer will create greater movement.

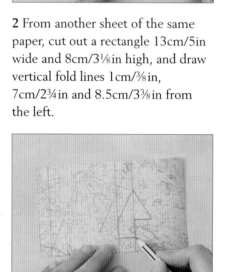

2 From another sheet of the same paper, cut out a rectangle 13cm/5in wide and 8cm/3⅛in high, and draw vertical fold lines 1cm/⅜in, 7cm/2¾in and 8.5cm/3⅜in from the left.

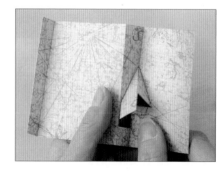

3 On the 8.5cm/3⅜in line, mark an A fold 3cm/1³⁄₁₆in wide and 2.5cm/1in high. Extend the left side of the A shape downwards 1–2cm/⅜–¾in to make a joining tab.

4 Indent all the fold lines and fold the verticals as shown. Cut the base line of the A fold, including the extension, and fold the A outwards from the back.

5 Attach the piece to the page at the tab markings, sticking first the right-hand tab, then the tab to the left. The piece should lie flat when the page is open and fold flat when closed.

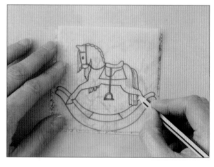

6 Draw the rocking horse on tracing paper (to fit into a 9cm/3½in square), then transfer the design to the patterned paper.

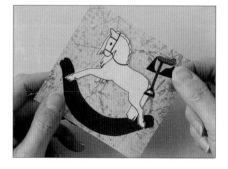

7 Paint the rocking horse or use the tracing to cut out the shapes from coloured papers and glue them on.

8 Cut around the shape and attach it to the extension of the A fold, being sure to glue only the extension and not the whole of the A fold. Experiment with the position of the horse using masking tape to get a good movement – the extension needs to be towards the bottom of the rocking horse.

TIP
Try adding a rider to the horse, which will increase the effect of the movement, but make sure that the design still fits inside the page when it is closed.

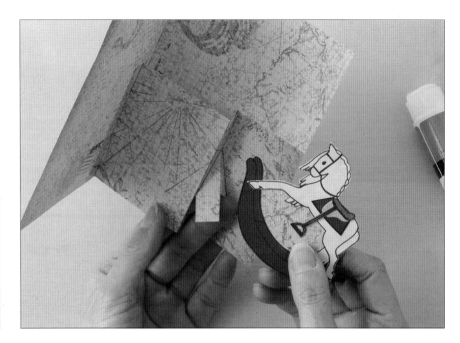

Rotating scene with hub

This technique allows a scene to be animated by rotating a disc hidden behind; it can be used for showing downwards or upwards movements, depending on where the viewing window is cut on the page.

MATERIALS AND EQUIPMENT
A4 white paper
metal ruler
pencil
cutting mat
craft knife
embossing tool
glue
pair of compasses
masking tape

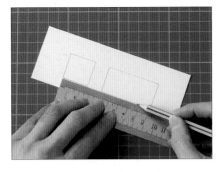

1 Begin by making the "hub" – the mechanism that enables the wheel to turn on the page. The quickest and easiest form to make is a square hub, consisting of two pieces: a 2.5cm/1in square (the washer), and the "split pin", made from a 2.5 x 5cm/1 x 2in rectangle folded in half.

TIP
This technique is ideal for simulating flowing water, falling snow or the flickering flames of a fire. The movement is governed by the direction in which the wheel is turned and also the positioning of the window – be it left, right, top or bottom.

2 Indent across the middle of the rectangle to create two squares. In one of the squares, cut two central legs, 5mm/³⁄₁₆in wide, leaving the centre uncut so that when the legs are folded up an H shape remains.

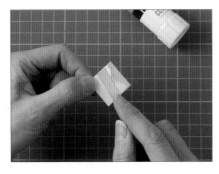

3 Fold the rectangle in half and glue it to make a square split pin. It is good to have a large area to attach to the page, but the square can be trimmed if it gets in the way.

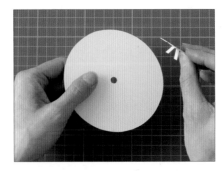

4 Draw and cut out a 10cm/4in diameter circle, then cut a 5mm/³⁄₁₆in hole in the centre. Push the legs of the split pin through the hole, then glue them to the square washer, so that the wheel spins freely in the "hub".

5 Cut a rectangle 21cm/8³⁄₈in wide and 10cm/4in high. Fold in a 1cm/³⁄₈in tab at one side, then fold the remaining card in half, to make a square with the folded tab to the right.

6 Leaving a margin of 1cm/³⁄₈in all the way round, cut out the front page and a curve on the folded tab side to allow access to the wheel, so that it can be spun manually.

7 For the inner panel that will hold the wheel, cut a rectangle 19cm/7½in wide and 9.5cm/3¾in high. Fold it in half with the open edge to the right, and cut a curve to match the larger outer card.

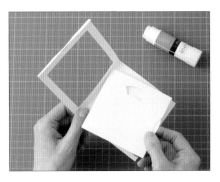

8 Draw a rough version of your image on scrap paper and cut out a window with the final effect of the movement in mind.

9 Attach the wheel and hub to the inner panel. Draw the image on the wheel through the window, turning it so the image travels around the wheel.

10 When the design is complete, attach the hub permanently to the inner panel and glue the inner panel inside the cover.

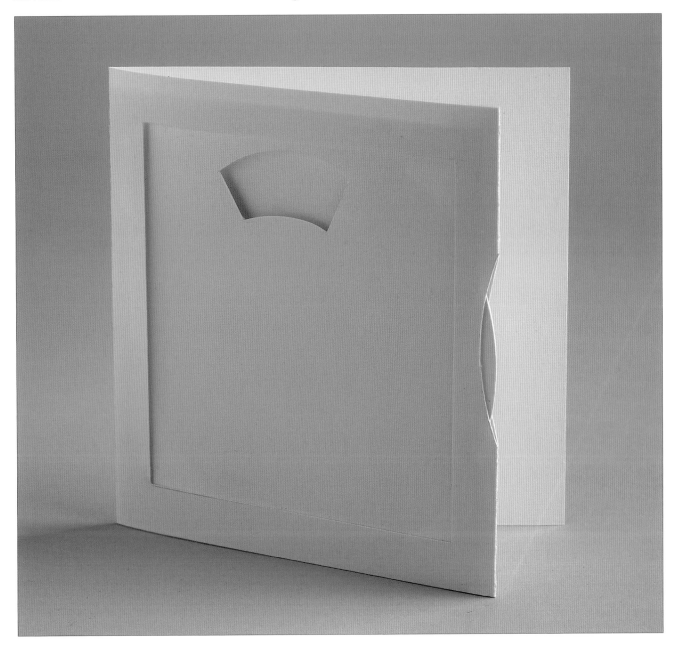

Watering can

This image makes full use of the downward movement of the disc, creating an everlasting watering can.

MATERIALS AND EQUIPMENT
A4 thin card (stock) in white and blue
metal ruler
pencil
cutting mat
craft knife
bone folder
glue
pair of compasses
patterned card (stock)
silver pen
coloured paper

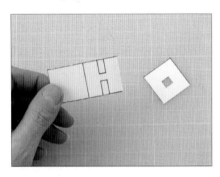

1 Begin by making the "hub". It is made of two pieces: a 2.5cm/1in square (the washer), and the "split pin", made from a 2.5 x 5cm/1 x 2in rectangle folded in half.

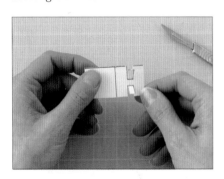

2 Indent across the middle of the rectangle. In one half cut two central legs, 5mm/³⁄₁₆in wide, leaving the centre uncut so that when the legs are folded up an H-shape remains.

3 Fold the rectangle in half and glue, leaving you with a square split pin.

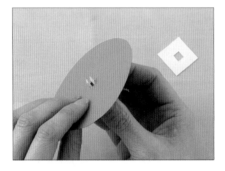

4 Draw and cut out a 10cm/4in diameter circle on blue paper, then cut a 5mm/³⁄₁₆in hole in the centre. Push the legs of the split pin through the hole, then glue them to the washer, so that the wheel spins freely in the hub.

5 The outer card is made from a 21cm x 10cm/8½in x 4in rectangle, cut from patterned card. With the long edge toward you, fold a tab of 1cm/½in down the right-hand side, then fold the remaining card in half. This will result in a square shape with the folded tab to the right.

6 Leaving a margin of 1cm/⅜in all the way round, cut shutters into the front page and indent their edges so that they open freely. Cut a curve into the folded tab side to allow access to manually spin the wheel.

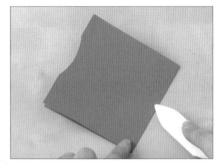

7 The inner panel will hold the wheel. This is a rectangle of 19cm/7½in wide x 9.5cm/4in high folded in half, with the open edge to the right. Cut a matching curve as with the outer card tab.

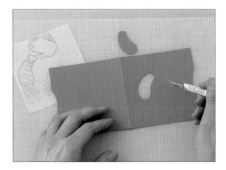

8 Draw a rough version of your image on scrap paper and cut out a window with the position of the movement in mind. Transfer your design to the front of the inner panel.

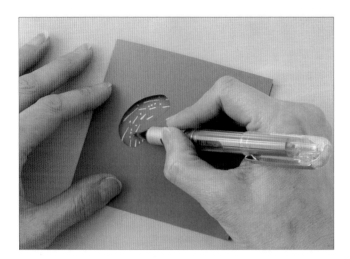

9 Attach the wheel and hub to the inner panel. Draw the image on the wheel through the window with the silver pen, turning it so the image goes around the wheel.

10 Complete your design in coloured paper. Once finished, permanently attach the hub to the inner panel and glue the inner panel inside the cover.

Complex projects

The projects in this chapter are more complicated than those elsewhere in the book, and you will need to draw on the skills you have already learned to complete them. These pop-ups may look slightly more demanding, but they draw on the same basic techniques that you have already mastered.

They will need more of an investment of time, but the results are so special that it is well worth making the effort to achieve them.

Included here are a magnificent Chinese dragon, a whimsical, spinning merry-go-round, a beautiful jungle with swinging monkeys, and a decorative pond with jumping frog and fish.

Starfish

This friendly-looking sea creature is a fun variation on multiple A and V folds on layers, a very easy technique that creates lots of movement. A few simple swirls on the background are all that is needed to suggest an aquatic setting, although you could add more detail if you want to create the feeling of an underwater kingdom.

MATERIALS AND EQUIPMENT
A4 coloured and patterned paper or
    thin card (stock)
bone folder
metal ruler
pencil
cutting mat
craft knife
tracing paper
protractor
embossing tool
glue
felt-tipped pens
scraps of shiny paper

2 On tracing paper, draw the body of the starfish 15cm/6in high and 7cm/2¾in wide, and add 8cm/3⅛in vertical tabs to each side. Draw two vertical lines with a 45° V and A (2cm/¾in apart) on each, and using these as guides draw two legs on each line, one pair leaning to the left and the other to the right. Each leg will be about 9cm/3½in long.

1 Fold a coloured or patterned sheet in half widthways for the background (A4 is a good size, but here we have used a larger piece to get extra height for the papercut decoration at the top). Cut 8cm/3⅛in vertical tab slits 3.5cm/1⅜in from the spine on each side, starting 5cm/2in from the bottom.

3 Transfer the designs to a coloured or patterned sheet.

4 Cut out the pairs of legs and the body.

5 Indent the spine fold and tab folds on the body, and the A and V folds on the legs. Fold the indented spine and tabs on the body.

TIP
The legs could be attached as a single piece, as long as they match the width of the body.

6 Slide the tabs on the body of the starfish into the vertical slits in the background, and glue them on to the back.

7 Fold the A and V folds on the legs and glue to the body and the background using the central tab areas only.

8 Add the finishing touches of the eyes and mouth, and decorate the background with a few swirling shapes cut from shiny paper.

Panda

This is a combination of two V folds, which produce the arm movements, and a layer, which hides one of the mechanisms. Try varying the V folds to As to achieve different movements, such as making one arm move upwards while the other goes down.

MATERIALS AND EQUIPMENT
A4 coloured and white paper
bone folder
metal ruler
pencil
felt-tipped pens
cutting mat
craft knife
embossing tool
glue

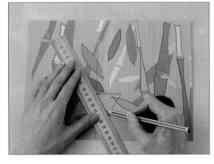

1 Fold an A4 sheet in half widthways for the background. This can be plain or decorated, but you will need to draw one of the panda's legs on the right-hand page. Mark a 15cm/6in tab position 2cm/¾in to the left of the spine, starting at the bottom. Draw a V fold 4cm/1½in up from the bottom of the spine, 3.5cm/1⅜in high and 4cm/1½in wide, and cut the top horizontal line to enable it to move.

TIP
The movement of the arm on the left-hand page can be reversed by using an A (rather than a V) fold.

2 On a white sheet, draw the panda's head and body. Mark a vertical fold line 7cm/2¾in from the left edge, and on this mark a V fold 1cm/⅜in up from the bottom, 3.5cm/1⅜in high and 4cm/1½in wide. The panda's head should extend no more than 6cm/2¼in to the right of the fold, and the body no more than 12cm/4¾in.

3 On the same sheet draw two arms, and colour in all the parts. Draw a support leg (a 2cm/¾in square with 1cm/⅜in tabs left and right) to hold the panda to the page on the right.

4 Indent the fold lines on all of the pieces. Cut out the shapes and cut across the top of the V fold as before.

5 Fold the background page at the spine, and push the V fold outwards from the back.

6 Open out the background page and securely attach the back arm to the V fold.

7 Next, glue the left-hand part of the body to the background, carefully aligning the fold with the tab marking. Glue the support leg under the body at the bottom right.

8 Glue the remaining arm to the V fold on the layer. As a final touch, attach a bunch of bamboo shoots to the back arm – this is best done at the end so you can check it is at the right angle to reach the panda's mouth. You may need to add a mountain fold so that it dips towards the page and doesn't miss the mouth entirely.

▲ *As you open and close the card, the panda's arm will move to its mouth, as if it is chomping on a feast of tasty bamboo.*

The hungry wolf

This is a combination of a reverse A fold and a layer, which is very useful as the layer masks the A-fold mechanism, leaving only the moving pop-up showing. The design is based on a story of a wolf visiting the doctor, but the disappearing character could be Red Riding Hood or her grandmother.

MATERIALS AND EQUIPMENT
A4 paper or thin card (stock)
bone folder
metal ruler
pencil
felt-tipped pens
textured paper and paper scraps
  (optional)
glue
cutting mat
embossing tool
craft knife

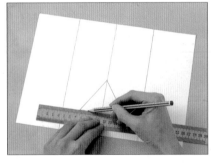

1 Fold an A4 sheet in half widthways and open out. Mark vertical tab positions for the layer 7cm/2¾in from the spine on each side. Approximately 4cm/1½in from the bottom of the spine, mark the add-on A-fold mechanism – a triangle 8cm/3⅛in wide and 6cm/2¼in high, plus an inner triangle on the same base line, 3cm/1³⁄₁₆in wide and 2.5cm/1in high.

2 Colour in the section within the tab lines, which will be the inside of the wolf's mouth (the rest of the sheet will be hidden). Redraw the A-fold triangles if necessary.

3 On a separate sheet (which will be the top layer), draw vertical fold lines in the centre and 7cm/2¾in to either side. Draw the wolf's open jaws within the two outer lines, with the rest of the head and the neck outside them. Colour in your design, or cut the details out of paper and glue them on.

TIPS
• If you would like to experiment with the central figure, remember that wider angles create a greater movement.
• When gluing the figure on to the mechanism, try to avoid gluing the central spine on both; this area needs to be able to move, so glue to the sides only.

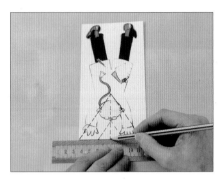

4 Next draw and colour in the character to be swallowed, about 15cm/6in high in total. Indent a vertical central fold, and on this lightly draw the A-fold mechanism from step 1 as a guide to positioning.

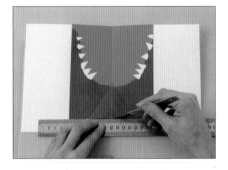

5 Draw the same inner triangle within the marked triangle on the base page, indent the fold lines and cut across the horizontal base of the A fold.

6 Indent the fold lines on the top layer and cut out all the pieces. Fold the A-fold mechanism outwards, then reverse-fold the inner section. Crease the vertical folds in the figure and the top layer.

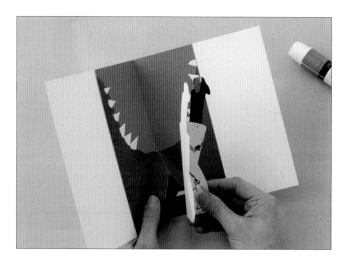

7 Glue the base of the figure to the inverted inner A fold, following the pencilled guidelines.

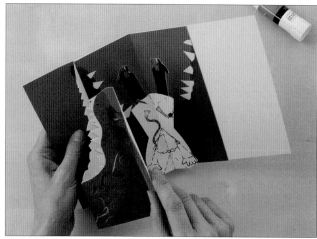

8 Place the top layer with the wolf's jaws over this and attach to the tab markings on the page, checking that all is working before gluing permanently.

Monkeys in a tree

This little scene is a combination of a reverse A fold underneath a layer, which produces a large sideways sweeping movement that can go right off the page: just right for cheeky monkeys swinging through the jungle.

MATERIALS AND EQUIPMENT
A5 white thin card (stock) or thick paper
bone folder
metal ruler
pencil
felt-tipped pens
cutting mat
craft knife
embossing tool
masking tape
glue

3 Fold a second A5 sheet in half widthways, and draw trees down the length of the spine. The design can reach almost to the edge of the left-hand page; the main trunk should overlap 1.5cm/⁹⁄₁₆in on to the right-hand page, and the leaves above should extend to 7cm/2¾in from the spine. Colour and cut out.

1 Fold an A5 sheet in half widthways and unfold. Mark a tab position 1.5cm/⁹⁄₁₆in to the left of the spine, and another 3cm/1³⁄₁₆in long at the top of the page, 6cm/2¼in to the right of the spine.

4 Now for the monkeys: monkey 1 hangs from a tab 10 x 3cm/4 x 1³⁄₁₆in, with vertical fold lines at 1cm/³⁄₈in, 7cm/2¾in and 8.5cm/3⁵⁄₁₆in. Allow a little extra on the right to shape into leaves. Draw an A fold on the 7cm/2¾in line (2cm/¾in high and 3cm/1³⁄₁₆in wide) with the monkey hanging from its right side. Monkey 2 hangs from the left side of an A fold on a tab 7 x 3cm/2¾ x 1³⁄₁₆in, with vertical folds at 1cm/³⁄₈in, 2.5cm/1in and 4cm/1½in. Monkey 3 reaches up from the left side of a V fold that is the same size as the others, on a tab 3cm/1³⁄₁₆in square. Colour in.

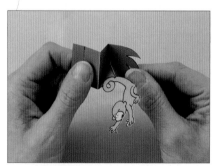

5 Cut out the monkeys on their tabs, indent all the fold lines on the tree layer and the monkeys, and crease.

2 Design and colour in a jungle background with plenty of trees.

6 Glue the left side of the tree layer at the marked position on the left side of the background.

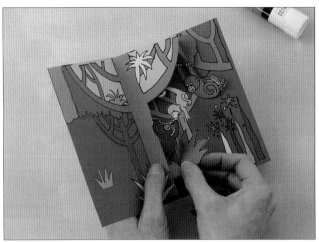

7 On the back of the tree layer, using masking tape first, attach monkey 1 approximately 1cm/⅜in from the outer edge, followed by monkey 2 about halfway along, then attach the other end of the tabs to the right-hand page.

8 Finally, attach monkey 3 to the spine at the bottom of the page, tucked behind the layer. When all three monkeys are co-ordinated and in the right positions (they may need some adjusting), glue them in place permanently.

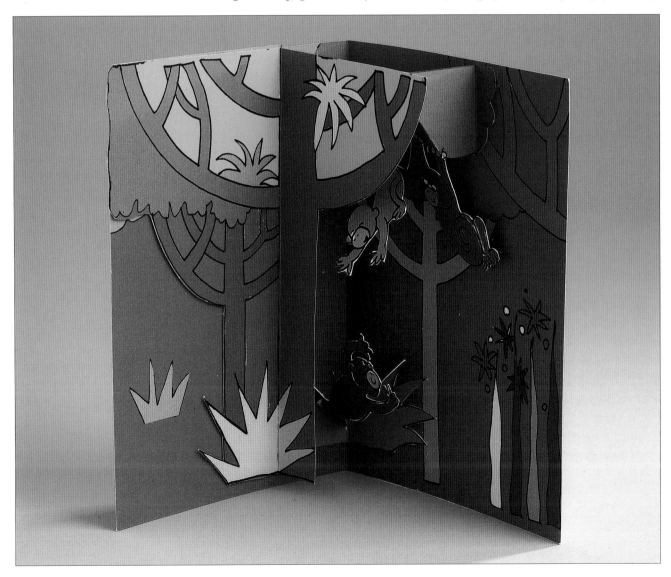

Pirates ahoy!

This project uses the layer fold, but introduces an articulated body to produce great movement. You could add even more movement by making the boat a shallow layer in itself. If you want to disguise the metal paper fasteners needed for this design, cover them with paper.

MATERIALS AND EQUIPMENT
A4 thin card (stock) or thick paper
bone folder
metal ruler
pencil
felt-tipped pens
cutting mat
craft knife
embossing tool
small piece of thick card (stock) (optional)
glue
masking tape
3 metal paper fasteners
A4 tracing paper

1 Fold an A4 sheet of card or paper in half widthways and open out. Mark a 1.5cm/⁹⁄₁₆in vertical slit for a tab 1.5cm/⁹⁄₁₆in to the left of the spine and 9cm/3½in from the top, and mark another 13cm/5in long 3cm/1³⁄₁₆in to the left of the spine, starting at the bottom. Mark a point for the main pivot 7cm/2¾in to the right of the spine and 8cm/3⅛in from the bottom of the page.

2 Draw and colour in the background design of the waves and boat on the right-hand page. The left side of the boat should reach the spine.

3 Cut a horizontal slit for the figure to move, about three-quarters the length of the front of the boat, and another for the oar, which should be 4cm/1½in below the pivot hole and 5cm/2in long: cut this following the wave. At the bottom, mark vertical tab positions for the second boat, 4cm/1½in to the left of the spine and 9.5cm/3¾in to the right.

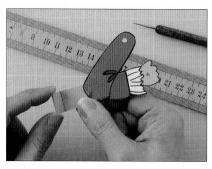

4 Draw the pirate's arm, which is the main tab pull and pivoting arm. The lower half is based on a horizontal strip 9 x 1.5cm/3½ x ⁹⁄₁₆in. Mark a vertical fold for the tab 1cm/⅜in from the left end. Add the top half of the arm (the same length as the lower part – approximately 6cm/2¼in) at an angle. Indent the tab fold and make small holes at the hand and shoulder. Colour and cut the piece out.

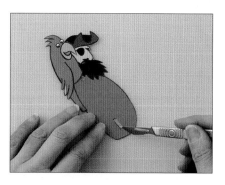

5 Draw, colour in and cut out the head and the top half of the body, about 12cm/4¾in long and of any width. Cut a 2cm/¾in slit, starting 1.5cm/⁹⁄₁₆in from the bottom, for a paper fastener to allow movement, then use the arm as a guide to make a hole in the shoulder joint.

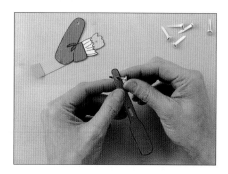

6 The final moving part is the oar, which will be shaped from a 10 x 2cm/4 x ¾in strip. It needs to be strong, so use a double layer or cut it from thicker card. Cut a pivot slit about halfway down that is identical to the one in the body, and make a hole 1.5cm/⁹⁄₁₆in from the top.

> **TIP**
> For a cleaner look you could make your own fasteners out of paper. The technique for achieving this is described in the 'Rotating scene with hub' project on pages 138–9.

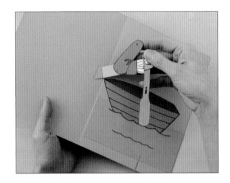

7 Now insert the pull tab arm in the left page slot and secure it at the back. Check the movement then attach the oar to the hand with a paper fastener and slide the bottom of the oar into the water slot.

8 Slide the body into the slit in the boat and connect the arm to the body at the shoulder joint.

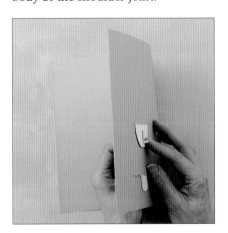

9 Line up the slots on the body and the oar, with the pivot hole on the page in between, and connect all three with a paper fastener.

10 Draw the layer showing the second boat within a rectangle 17cm/6⅝in wide and 20cm/8in high, with vertical fold lines at 2cm/¾in, 11cm/4⅜in and 14cm/5½in from the left. (It is easier to draw this on tracing paper first – place it over the page and draw the fold lines in line with the tab markings.)

11 Indent and fold the vertical lines, although if you want the water base to fold and not the boat's prow, as shown, finalize the design before folding the front corner of the layer.

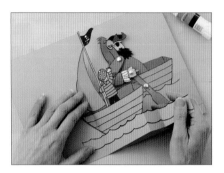

12 Glue the layer to the tab positions marked on the page to complete the scene.

Chinese dragon

This very dramatic dragon pops right out of the page, but it is in fact quite a simple construction based on multiple A and V folds. It looks stunning on a bright gold background, but to save any mistakes on good paper and finished artwork, make a white dummy from your completed tracings to test first.

MATERIALS AND EQUIPMENT

A4 tracing paper
protractor
pencil
metal ruler
A4 thick paper or thin card (stock)
paints or felt-tipped pens
cutting mat
embossing tool
craft knife
bone folder
A4 gold card
glue
masking tape

TIP
Here is an alternative way to test the pop-up pieces will fit into the folded page (from step 2 onwards). Once the image is drawn on to the second piece of tracing paper, flip the sheet over and line up the angled line with the one on the first sheet. You will see where the image will sit in the page when folded. If it doesn't fit, keep the tracing paper in the same position and mark the edges of the page underneath. This will give you a guideline to keep within when re-drawing the dragon.

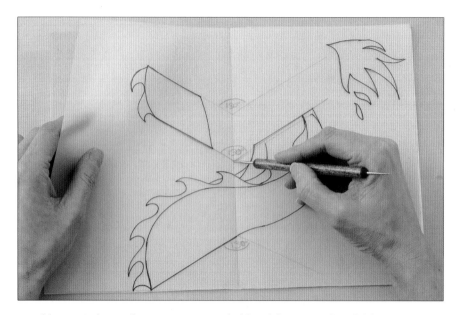

1 Fold an A4 sheet of tracing paper in half widthways and unfold. From a point 7cm/2¾in from the top of the spine, draw a V with 8cm/3⅛in arms at 60° on either side. Draw an identical V 4cm/1½in below this. Starting 4cm/1½in from the bottom, draw an A with an angle of 60° on the left and 65° on the right, extending to the bottom of the page. Visualizing the dragon snaking in an S shape, draw the areas where it will be flat on the background page: between the Vs on the left, and from the right of the middle V to the left of the bottom A. Add flames emerging from the mouth.

2 On another sheet of tracing paper, draw a spine and a V fold with angles of 65° on both sides. Line up the left arm of the V with the left arm of the top V on the background, and draw the dragon's neck and head curving round to reach the right side of the V. Add tabs disguised as the forelegs below the V on either side.

3 Draw the tail and a lower leg as one piece in the same way, using an A with an angle of 60° on the left and 65° on the right. Test that the tail will fit into the closed page by folding the drawing and lining it up with the folded page, so that you can see if any adjustments are necessary.

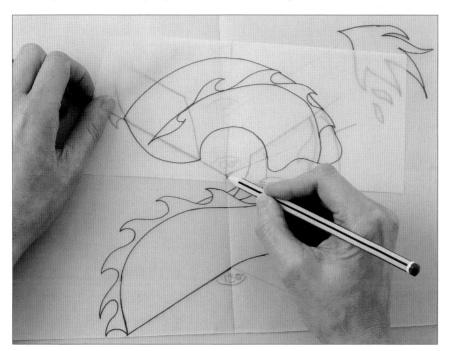

4 Base the middle section on a V with angles of 65° on each side. Line up the left arm with the lower V on the background page and draw a rough curve around to the right arm, then change the position of the top sheet to line up the right arms of the Vs, and adjust the body thickness until it matches the background. Add tabs for attaching to the page as before.

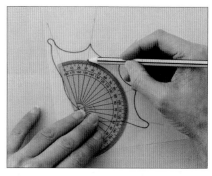

5 The wing is made up of four sections of 30° with tabs on each end, looking rather like an umbrella. Draw it no larger than 7 cm/2¾ in from centre to tips, so that it will not get in the way of the tail when closing the page.

6 Transfer the drawings of all the pieces on to thick paper or thin card, including the sections that will be flat on the background page. Colour them in, and indent the folds in the moving parts before cutting out. Take care with the tail: fold the spine only at the body end and not in the length, so it creates a swooping effect as it is opened.

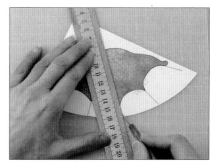

7 Indent the fold lines in the wing before cutting out.

8 Fold each indented line of the wing accordion-fashion.

9 Make a centre fold in an A4 sheet of gold card. Glue the static body pieces to the background page in the same positions as in the original drawing. Attach the head section, lining up both tabs with the top V on the background – the different angles on the background and the pop-up will make it stand up well.

10 Add the middle section of the body, lining up the tabs with the lower V.

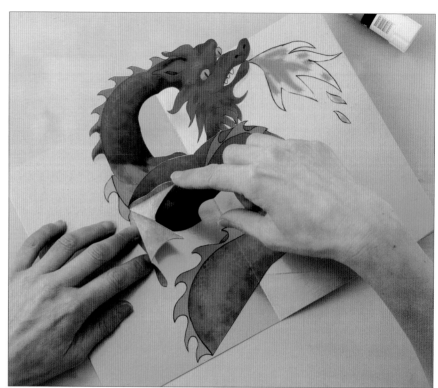

11 Attach one side of the folded dragon's wing to the background page and the other to the pop-up body section: test this first by sticking with masking tape and closing the page to get the correct position. When you are happy with the positioning, glue the wing in place.

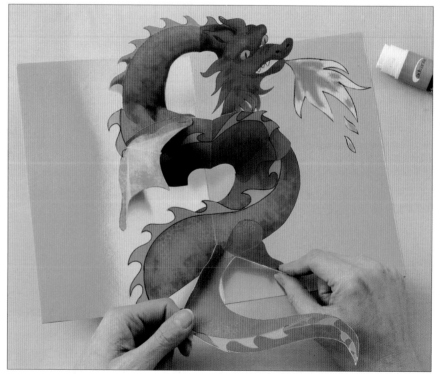

12 Finally, add the tail, gluing the tabs along the lines of the A at the bottom of the page.

Bobbing seagulls

This project uses layers, but also introduces a dangling technique, where the dangling mechanism is hidden away. It creates a fun rocking movement in the section above it. This is a cheerful nautical-themed card, which features the view through a ship's porthole of resting seagulls bobbing gently on the rolling waves.

MATERIALS AND EQUIPMENT
A4 thick paper or thin card (stock) in pale blue, red, blue and white
bone folder
metal ruler
pencil
cutting mat
embossing tool
craft knife
pair of compasses
small piece of stiff cardboard
masking tape
glue
felt-tipped pens

1 Fold an A4 sheet in half widthways and unfold. Mark a point for the mechanism on the right-hand page, 4.5cm/1¾in from the spine and 8cm/3⅛in up from the bottom.

2 Mark three 16cm/6⅜in vertical tab positions, starting at the bottom: 4cm/1½in and 5cm/2in to the left of the spine and 9cm3½in to the right.

3 For the porthole layer, draw a rectangle 14cm/5½in wide and 16cm/6⅜in high on coloured paper. Add a 1cm/⅜in tab down each side, and indent a vertical fold line 9cm/3½in from the left. Indent the fold lines and cut out the outline with a craft knife.

4 For the porthole on the front of the layer, draw and cut out a 6cm/2¼in-radius circle with its centre 8cm/3⅛in from the top. Add a strip of blue waves to the back and a decorative frame to the front. (If you wish, trim the side tabs to 12cm/4¾in long, and cut slits in the background page so that they can be pushed through and secured at the back.)

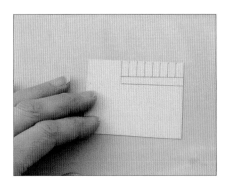

5 Use a piece of stiff cardboard to make the holding panel for the dangling sections. Draw a rectangle 4 x 1.5cm/1½ x ⁹⁄₁₆in, and from the top draw 1cm/³⁄₈in vertical lines every 5mm/³⁄₁₆in. The bottom 5mm/³⁄₁₆in will remain uncut and will be the main support.

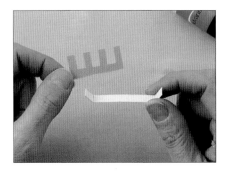

6 Cut out each alternate vertical, leaving four pegs which will separate the pieces. Cut a 6cm/2¼in strip of thin card 5mm/³⁄₁₆in wide, indent 1cm/³⁄₈in at each end and glue this to the thicker cardboard, so that the piece now has tabs attached.

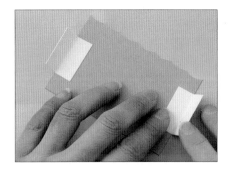

7 To make the inner wave layer, to which the support will be attached, cut out a blue rectangle 13cm/5in wide and cut waves across the top. Add 1cm/³⁄₈in tabs at either end.

8 Construct the four moving parts using blue card: the wave pieces are 6cm/2¼in wide and 5cm/2in high. Lightly draw a wavy top edge to simulate the sea on each of the pieces and cut along the edges carefully with a craft knife.

9 Draw the floating seagulls, making each one 2cm/³⁄₄in high. Colour them in with felt-tipped pens and glue them (by their feet) to two of the wave panels. Mark a central point on each piece, 4cm/1½in up from the long bottom edge of the blue card.

10 From the marked point downwards, cut out an oval in the centre of each panel, which will rest on the holding bar. Above this cut a small downward-facing crescent, through which the top securing bar will pass.

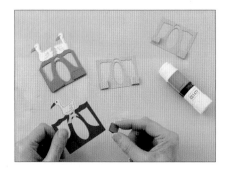

11 Cut out the upper side sections that will not be in view, to reduce the weight in the middle, and add a few layers of card to the bottom outer corners to add weight to each panel.

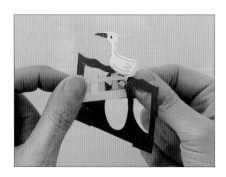

12 Cut a length of card 4cm/1½in long and 5mm/³⁄₁₆in wide. As you slip the wave sections on to the holding bar, slide the length of card through the small crescents and glue the ends to the bar, so that the pieces are enclosed but move freely when wobbled.

13 Attach the front tab of the holding bar to the inner wave layer and glue the left tab of the layer to the left page at the inner tab marking. Glue the back of the holding bar to the right-hand page at the marked point.

14 Next, attach the porthole layer to the outer marking on the left-hand page. Attach the layer holding the moving parts to the right-hand side of the porthole layer 1cm/³⁄₈in behind the corner fold. Use tape to secure everything until the final step, so that the mechanism can be tested and adjusted if necessary.

15 Slot the right-hand side of the porthole layer into the slit on the background page and secure at the back. When the card is moved gently from side to side, the gulls will bob up and down on the sea. Check that all is working well, then secure permanently with glue.

TIP
The secret of the stunning rocking movement is the weight distribution in the moving parts: there must be more weight on the bottom outside corners of each panel and minimal weight in the middle. This is why you need to cut out as much as possible of the areas that will not be seen. If you do it gradually, hanging the sections on the holding bar, you can experiment with the movement produced.

Salmon's leap

This is a combination of layers, a V mechanism pulling a panel from a slot, and a variation on the pivot technique. Add to this a simple curved fold, and a beautiful three-dimensional shape emerges and moves as the page is opened.

MATERIALS AND EQUIPMENT
A4 pearlized and coloured card (stock)
A4 tracing paper
metal ruler
pencil
cutting mat
embossing tool
craft knife
bone folder
silver marker pen
masking tape
glue
medium-weight patterned paper
2 paper fasteners

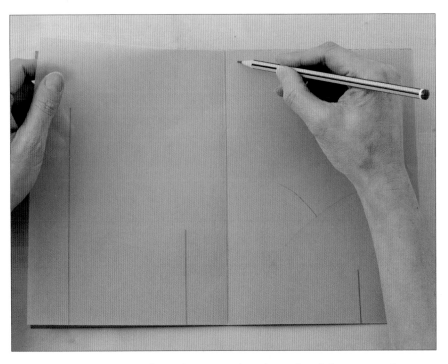

2 Mark a point 1cm/⅜in from the top and to the right of the spine, where the salmon's head will be attached. For the tall waterfall layer, draw a 16cm/6⅜in vertical tab position 3cm/1³⁄₁₆in from the edge of the left page.

1 Fold an A4 sheet of stiff blue card in half widthways for the background and unfold. (If you are using pearlized card, draw the design on tracing paper first to avoid spoiling the surface.) For the layer at the bottom of the page, draw a 7cm/2¾in vertical tab line 3cm/1³⁄₁₆in to the left of the spine and another 4cm/1½in line 10cm/4in to the right.

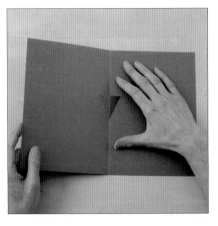

3 Make a V fold, beginning 9cm/3½in from the bottom of the spine, 4cm/1½in high and 4cm/1½in wide.

> **TIP**
> A hand-illustrated version of this would be stunning. Make up the project on white paper first to use as a template for your design.

4 Cut a curved diagonal slot, beginning 4cm/1½in from the bottom of the page and 3cm/1³⁄₁₆in to the right of the spine. The slot should be approximately 6cm/2¼in long, although it may need to be longer. This will depend on the size of the "splash" panel you make.

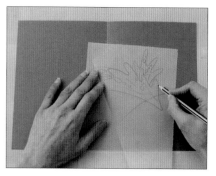

7 To make the splash panel to fit the V mechanism, place a sheet of tracing paper on the page and draw a curved splash between the left side of the V fold and the slot, adding enough extra length to keep it anchored in the slot. Transfer the design to card and decorate it as before. Mark a point where the base of the salmon will attach (see Tip).

5 Next, draw the water panels, working on tracing paper first. The base layer is the foundation for the waterfall, so begin with this, drawing a curved splash 16cm/6⅜in wide and 8cm/3⅛in high. It needs a 10cm/4in front panel, a 3cm/1³⁄₁₆in side panel and 1.5cm/⁹⁄₁₆in tabs on each end. Add a vertical tab position 2cm/¾in in from the left of the front panel, for the waterfall.

TIP
The salmon needs to be attached to the splash at a point that will be above the slot when the page is closed. Find this by holding a pencil point on the tracing at the slot, then rotate the tracing, holding it at the spine, until the top left of the splash reaches the right-hand side of the V fold. You can now mark the point above the slot.

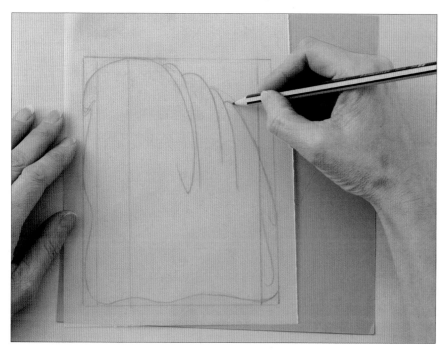

6 Draw the waterfall within an area 16cm/6⅜in high and 12.5cm/4⅞in wide, including a 2cm/¾in side panel, 8.5cm/3⁵⁄₁₆in front panel and 1cm/⅜in tabs each side. Transfer the water designs to light blue card and decorate them – for this card papercuts have been used to add depth and another dimension.

8 Assemble the layers before making the salmon. Cut out the splash and attach it to the left side of the V fold, using masking tape initially, and test to see that it slides easily as the page is opened.

9 Indent all fold lines and cut out the base panel, then attach it to the left page only, at the tab marking. Do the same with the waterfall panel, attaching it to the left page and the marking on the base panel.

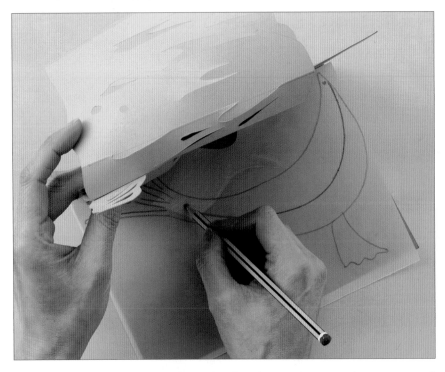

10 Place a sheet of tracing paper in the closed page (cut away the area around the V fold to get a flat surface for drawing), open the page slightly and mark the two attachment points at the salmon's head and tail. Around these, draw a curved salmon with a central spine running along its length: it should be no longer than 20cm/8in to keep it within the page.

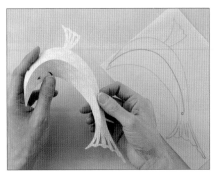

11 Transfer the design to medium-weight paper and decorate, then score the curved spine with a craft knife, cut out the salmon and gently fold along the curve of the spine.

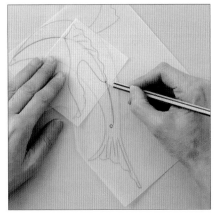

12 The top fin and left fin are separate, to add to the three-dimensional effect. Place tracing paper over the salmon design to draw the two fins, and connect as one piece. Transfer and cut out.

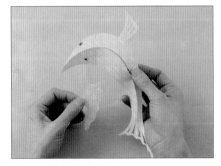

13 Mark the position where the top fin will fit on the spine and cut a slot, then slide the fin piece in and secure underneath with tape or glue. Cut slits at the top and bottom markings for the paper fasteners.

14 Attach the salmon to the top of the page and to the splash. Test the movement by folding the card – you may need to adjust the positions of the holes to get it right. Glue all the layers in place. Add a backing sheet to cover the holes, taking care not to glue the section below the slot.

TIP
A gentle movement is needed to create the natural curve of the fish, so attach carefully. If it is too forced the fish will crease and fold.

Jumping fish and frog

The design of this dynamic card is all about action and reaction. As the big fish comes to the surface of this crowded pond, the tiny minnows leap from the water and the cautious frog disappears under the water. All the movements are produced using the same basic technique: A and V folds, which are hidden from view by decorative lily pads.

MATERIALS AND EQUIPMENT
A4 thin white card (stock) and
    coloured paper
bone folder
felt-tipped pens or paints
metal ruler
pencil
tracing paper
cutting mat
embossing tool
craft knife
glue
small piece of thick card
masking tape

TIP
A- and V-fold mechanisms have been covered previously; here the reverse A fold has an extension added to it to offer a larger area for gluing on the pop-up. To achieve the same effect as shown, the mechanism has been cut from the corner of the paper.

1 Fold a sheet of A4 card in half widthways and open out. Decorate the background and glue on a strip of coloured paper 11cm/4⅜in wide for the pond water foreground. Mark 10cm/4in vertical tab positions starting at the bottom of the page, 7cm/2¾in to each side of the spine.

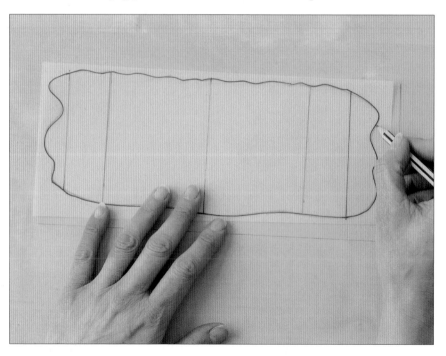

2 Draw the base layer on tracing paper, 22cm/8¾in wide and 10cm/4in high. Draw fold lines 1cm/⅜in and 4cm/1½in in from each side and mark a central spine. Transfer the design to coloured paper.

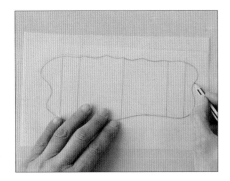

3 Draw the next layer on tracing paper, 16cm/6⅜in wide and 8cm/3⅛in high. This also needs a central fold, 1cm/⅜in tab folds on each side and further folds 3cm/1³⁄₁₆in in from each side. Transfer to coloured paper, indent the fold lines on both pieces and cut out.

4 Make three mechanisms for the moving parts: two V folds and one reverse A fold, each 5cm/2in wide and 3cm/1³⁄₁₆in high. Cut and fold these, ready to attach the pop-up pieces.

5 On thin white card, draw the head of the big fish, no larger than 5cm/2in long, the pair of jumping fish, around 7cm/2¾in long, and the frog in a similar size. Colour these in and add a curved arm to the base of the jumping fish.

6 Cut out the coloured pieces and the layers, and indent and fold the marked lines.

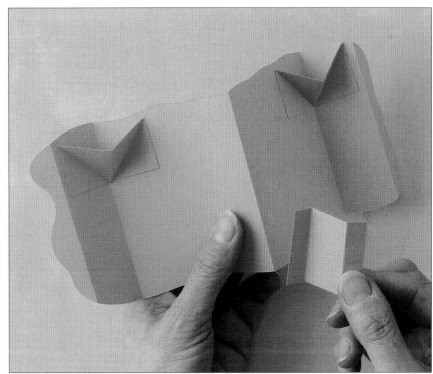

7 On the back of the base layer, glue the two V-fold mechanisms at the 4cm/1½in folds, close to the top. This layer will need additional support, so cut out a tabbed leg from thicker card, to hold the layer 3cm/1³⁄₁₆in from the page at the spine.

8 Glue the layer to the page, attaching the leg support you have just made in the centre and attaching the two side tabs at the marked positions.

10 Now, add the characters to the mechanisms, securing them with masking tape to test their positions before gluing.

9 Glue the reverse A-fold mechanism to the centre front of the layer.

11 Draw, colour in and cut out lily leaves and a flower, and use them to decorate the second layer (the flower is a disguised V fold added to the centre fold).

12 Glue the side tabs of this layer to the base layer. Add more decorations to the page and layers if you like, but take care that they do not protrude from the closed page.

TIP
The pond could be awash with lily pads and they could form an intricate three-dimensional pattern across the multiple layers, so long as they are tested for size to ensure they are hidden when the card is closed.

Merry-go-round

This colourful fairground ride doesn't pop up by itself; the project is stored flat and needs some simple assembly, but it is worth it to see it spinning around. When dismantled it should all fit into a stout folded A4 card, so it's easy to send as a delightful surprise.

MATERIALS AND EQUIPMENT
stiff cardboard
circle cutter or pair of compasses
wooden skewer
A4 thin card (stock) and medium-
  weight paper in two contrasting
  colours and white
cutting mat
craft knife
metal ruler
pencil
protractor
embossing tool
bone folder
tracing paper
felt-tipped pens
glue
self-adhesive "jewels"

TIPS
• Do not use card that is too thick for this as it is quite small; if the card is too stiff the structure will not fold down well.
• This could be adapted to an up-pop mechanism with elastic stretched across the base (an example of this is shown in the Birthday Cake project on page 174 of this book). This would pull the structure open when released from the confines of the envelope.
• You could make a whole fairground scene, with several rides that are made to stay permanently open.

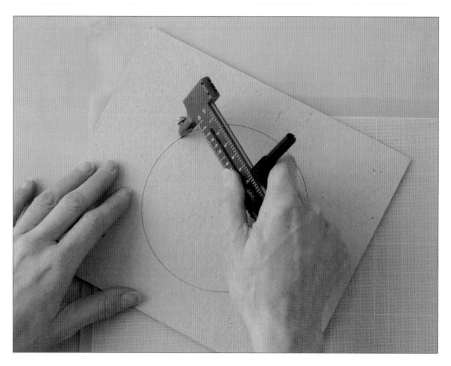

1 Cut out a 12cm/4¾in-diameter circle from cardboard for the base. Make a small hole in the centre, big enough to take a wooden skewer.

2 From coloured card, cut two circles 10cm/4in in diameter. Draw a fold line down the middle of one and on either side cut symmetrical slots 5mm/³⁄₁₆in, 3cm/1³⁄₁₆in and 4cm/1½in from the centre. These should get progressively longer: 5mm/³⁄₁₆in, 1cm/³⁄₈in and 1.5cm/⁹⁄₁₆in. Add a 3cm/1³⁄₁₆in slot about 1cm/³⁄₈in from the circumference, and cut a small hole in the centre.

3 Cut a small hole in the centre of the second circle, but don't fold it, as it is intended to keep the model from folding up when slotted together. Place it behind the first circle and mark the position of the slot near the edge, then draw and cut a curved slot that will fit the pieces together when the curve is slid through the straight slot.

5 Indent the lines between each section and indent straight lines across the scallops at the edge. Crease all the folds.

4 For the roof, use medium-weight paper, as card will be too stiff to fold well. Draw a 280° section of a 16cm/6⅜in-diameter circle and divide it into 14 sections of 20° each. At one side of the "missing" section add a tab to join the piece together. Draw a 14cm/5½in inner circle as a guide to draw a scalloped edge. Cut out the piece.

6 Repeat the roof design on paper in a contrasting colour, cut out individual sections and glue them to the roof to create stripes. You can do the same with the edges, but take care not to cover the fold.

7 Cut a 10 x 2.5cm/4 x 1in length of thin card and add the same symmetrical slots and fold line as on the circle in step 2.

8 To make the central pillar, draw on tracing paper a 5 x 3.5cm/2 x 1⅜in rectangle, and divide it vertically into seven sections. Add 1cm/⅜in tabs to the top and bottom of the third and fifth sections. Transfer on to medium-weight paper, cut out and indent the lines.

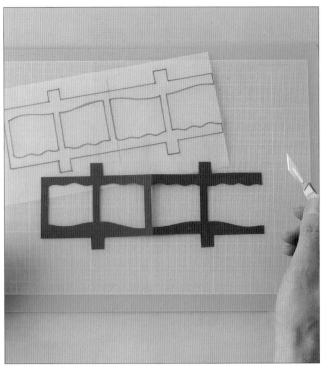

9 For the inner ring, draw an 18 x 5cm/7 x 5in rectangle. Divide this into four sections with pillars 5mm/³⁄₁₆in wide, adding 1cm/⅜in tabs above and below the second and fourth pillars. Draw a horizontal top piece and a floor, which can be straight or wavy. Add small gluing tabs to the open end to join the ring. Transfer on to coloured paper, indent a central fold line and cut out.

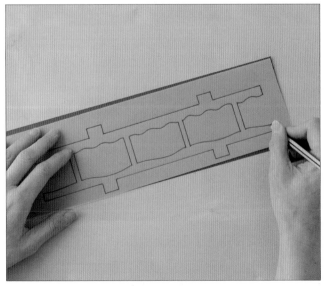

10 Make an outer ring in the same way, 24 x 5cm/9½ x 2in. Add top and bottom tabs 1.5cm/⁹⁄₁₆in wide, this time between the pillars. Add end tabs to one side, transfer on to paper and cut out.

11 Place a sheet of tracing paper over the rings and design an assortment of figures to fit on each pillar of the merry-go-round.

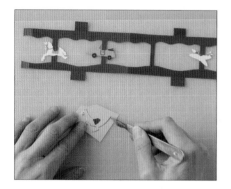

12 Transfer the designs on to different coloured papers, colour and cut out, then glue the pieces to the pillars. Glue the end tabs to join the rings and fold flat, lining up the top and bottom tabs.

13 Make a decorative surround for the base from a 2cm/¾in strip about 38cm/15in long – measure around the card base you have cut for the exact length, adding a tab. Indent a central fold and glue the ends together to form a ring.

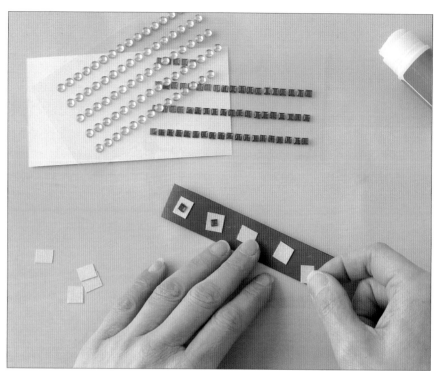

14 Decorate the ring with different colours and plastic "jewels" to look like coloured lights.

15 To assemble, fold the central pillar in half, lining up the top and bottom tabs, then glue the side tab. Fold the length from step 7 in half at the fold line and attach the top tabs of the pillar at the first slots. Attach the pillar to the corresponding slots in the circle base, and the inner and outer rings to the further sets of slots, attaching the top tabs of each ring to the slotted length.

16 Once the pillar and rings are attached at the top and bottom to the base and the holding length, glue the end tabs on this length and attach them to the inside of the roof.

18 To test, place the wooden skewer in the central hole on the base, fit the decorated strip around the base, place the merry-go-round on the skewer and spin.

17 The model is complete but will not stand up on its own until the second circle is attached. Slide the lip of the curved slot into the straight slot to line up the position, then release that side and glue the other halves of the circles together. Reconnect slots to assemble.

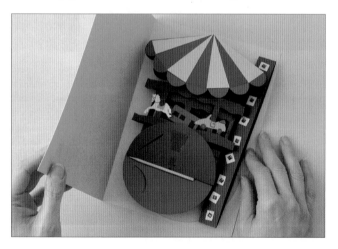

19 Disconnect the slots in the circles to fold the model flat; the pieces should all fit into a folded A4 card.

NOTE
The skewer will need to be cut to the right height – it should reach the holding strip at the top of the pillar while leaving a little clearance between the carousel and the base.

▶ *Once assembled the merry-go-round can easily be disassembled and laid flat inside a card.*

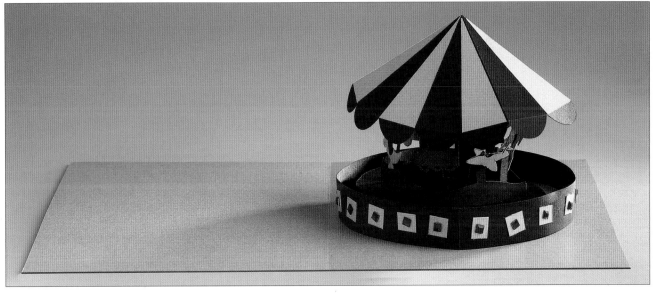

Index

Words in **bold** indicate projects.

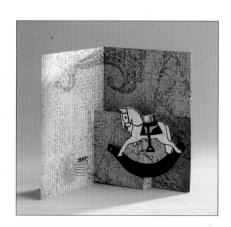